Settela

Settela

Aad Wagenaar

Translated by Janna Eliot

www.fiveleaves.co.uk

Settela

by Aad Wagenaar

Published in 2005
by Five Leaves Publications
PO Box 81, Nottingham NG5 4ER
info@fiveleaves.co.uk
www.fiveleaves.co.uk

Five Leaves acknowledges financial support
from Arts Council England

Design by 4 Sheets Design and Print
Printed in Great Britain

ISBN: 0 907123 70 8

Contents

Seven Seconds

The images only last seven seconds. Despite their short duration they amount to a complete film documentary of the deportation of Jews somewhere in Europe, to the extermination camps of the National Socialist Third Reich.

At first, we see part of the side of a goods wagon and the huge roundheaded clouts nailed into its vertical boards. Over the breadth of six planks, someone has chalked "74 Pers" in bold figures and flowing letters.

The camera goes up to the left, sweeps along a hand which seems to be bolting a door, and slants upwards to the knotted ends of a shawl. Then the camera comes to rest on the head and upper body of a young girl who is standing in the crack of the sliding door of the train wagon.

The door opening is roughly as large as one of the wall planks in the side of the train, the same size as the head of the young girl. Her head is covered with a light fabric and a trace of dark hair escapes beneath the headscarf; the face under the tightly pulled cloth is oval with deepset eyes. The girl's mouth is slightly open and her upper teeth can be seen.

The girl in the train wagon is looking out; for just under two seconds her eyes dart to and fro, to the left, to the right, to the left again, and then to the front to look down at something.

A slight shudder of fear runs through her upper body, as if she is tensing a shoulder, or being touched by someone in the wagon behind her.

When the seven seconds have elapsed, the film continues with other shots of the bustle which accompanies the departure of a long train, such as this one getting ready to leave the internment camp for Jews near the Drente village of Westerbork, on its way to the

1

concentration camps of Auschwitz, Sobibor, Bergen-Belsen or Theresienstadt.

It is the spring of 1944.

Prologue

Grevenbicht/Buchten
23rd December 1934

The nineteenth-century farmhouse on the Market Place of Grevenbicht had steadily acquired the magnificence of a town palace since Dr Victor Duysens and his wife Anna Maria had come to live there in 1919. Nearly every year extensions were added to both sides of the short driveway. Beyond the gate stretched a seemingly unending garden, where the doctor had his own tennis court and football field, and where his wife supervised the cultivation of vegetables, fruit and flowers. At the end of every autumn about four hundred plants were brought in from the garden to over-winter in the conservatory adjoining the turret room.

All the extensions and embellishments of the great forty-roomed house were due to the efforts of the doctor's wife. The almost constant building work in and around the house helped her combat the frequent feeling of emptiness caused by her daily life in the small village between Julianakanaal and Maas in the province of Limburg.

Life was completely different for her husband. As far as he was concerned, the days were never long enough. Victor Duysens, a forty-year old doctor, had, on 3rd December 1934, taken over his father-in-law's practice which included fifteen villages and hamlets in Limburg.

Although only ten kilometres from the town of Sittard, Grevenbicht was a backward area and immediately after settling in, Dr Duysens had his hands full combating child mortality.

After his morning surgery, during which he sometimes examined and treated as many as one hundred patients, Dr Duysens spent the afternoon visiting bedridden patients in his black De Soto car. Sometimes he stopped in the hamlets of the Land van Swentibold, holding his

3

surgery through the open car window, dispensing from the large box on the back seat of the car the pills, powders and salves which had been prepared by his servant Johan.

Anna Maria Duysens led her own life, hardly taking any part in her husband's busy practice. She was not a typical country doctor's wife and often pined for the excitement of a provincial capital, like Maastricht, — or the towns in the west of the country, Amsterdam, The Hague and Rotterdam — with their salons, theatres, and intellectual and artistic circles.

Anna Maria Elizabeth Geertruida Joosten, the daughter of a doctor from Sittard, was born on 19th November 1897. As a young girl she had been sent to a Maastricht boarding school for the daughters of well-off Limburg families, where the nuns gave the young women in their charge a broad education, a knowledge of arts and foreign languages and a thorough grounding in crafts such as painting, knitting and embroidery.

At the age of 18, Anna Maria Joosten, known as Annie, was said to be the most beautiful girl in town. Almost as soon as Victor Duysens made her acquaintance he asked her to marry him. Anna Maria Joosten, who had a lovely mezzosoprano voice and was about to audition in Rotterdam to be trained as a singer, succumbed to the advances of the polite up-and-coming general practitioner. After their wedding in Sittard Anna Maria followed her husband to Grevenbicht, where he took over the country practice and settled in the mansion on the Market Place. They lived there for over fifteen years and had three sons and one daughter. With motherhood Anna Maria became even more beautiful; at the age of thirty-seven she was a tall slim woman with gleaming black hair fastened in a bun. The natural grey streak in her dark hair lent a dignified beauty to her small face and brown eyes.

About three kilometers from Grevenbicht, along the country lane leading to the small church village of Buchten, lies

4

a pasture called Hitje. A small caravan with a high curved roof had been camped there for a few months, screened by pollard willows and thick reeds, with three windshields which kept hay dry for a horse. This was the home of Heinrich and Emilia Steinbach and their six children aged between two and twelve. They were part of an extensive Gypsy* family which, since the first Steinbachs had crossed the German border in the nineteenth century, had settled in a dozen encampments in the southern part of Limburg and regularly travelled from one camp to the other.

Heinrich, whose Gypsy name was Moeselman, supported his family through trading, but mainly earned his living making music as a violinist in all kinds of Gypsy orchestras — in cafés and at village festivals and fairs. Emilia, his wife, known as Toetela, sometimes peddled her goods round the Limburg villages, but spent most of her time caring for her family and the babies she bore every couple of years. By the end of December 1934, she was heavily pregnant again.

December was Anna Maria Duysens' favourite month. Some time before Christmas she placed a huge pine tree, sometimes five metres tall, in the enormous lower hall where it reached up to the very high ceiling. She spent so much time decorating the tree that it usually remained in the hall until Easter. Everyone from the village of Grevenbicht and beyond came to admire the exceptionally beautifully decorated Christmas tree, which was hung with sweets for children from poor families.

Of the many children welcomed into the doctor's house and grounds on the Market Place, there were a few Anna Maria was particularly pleased to see. These were the sons and daughters of the Gypsies who travelled through the

---

*The term *Gypsy* is used throughout, being a direct translation of *Zigeuner* in the original Dutch. See, however, the Afterword by Ian Hancock.

5

area in caravans or who camped in the neighbourhood, people like the Steinbachs who had stopped for some time in the nearby village of Buchten. No one in the village knew what she found so attractive about these children, unless it was their dark hair and beautiful light brown skin. But people gossiped about how the doctor's wife spoiled them, giving them food, sweets and garments, sometimes allowing them to play for up to half an hour in the big bathroom of her house.

There were dignitaries in Grevenbicht who disapproved of her involvement with the Gypsies, those *riffraff and beggars*. The pastor himself vented his wrath against them from the pulpit in one Sunday sermon. But he suffered for his words, because the following Monday Mrs Duysens drove to Roermond in her husband's De Soto — that was another shocking thing, a woman who could drive! — and complained to the Bishop of Limburg. The Bishop called the guardian of the Grevenbicht souls to his palace, reprimanded him and pointed out that Gypsies were also included amongst the people he was supposed to love as himself.

On Sunday 23 December a mild wind prevented the temperature from falling below zero and allowing Christmas Day its traditional trappings of frost and snow. The weather was cloudy and a little misty, more like autumn. But the decorated Christmas tree in the hall of the doctor's house was more beautiful than ever and laden more heavily with gifts than it had been the year before. Anna Maria Duysens sat in an armchair beside the tree wearing her best long black lace dress, playing the role of châtelaine, the lady of Grevenbicht castle.

As she received Christmas greetings and compliments on her pretty Christmas tree from the villagers that afternoon, the servant Johan brought in a message; a child had just been born in the Gypsy encampment at Hitje. Emilia Steinbach, who during her pregnancy had visited the Market Place a few times, had given birth to a girl. This

6

child, the doctor's wife was told, had been born in the open, under the caravan, in accordance with Gypsy custom, so it was fortunate that the real winter had not yet begun.

Along with the report of the birth, the doctor's wife received an entreaty from Moeselman and Toetela Steinbach, the parents of the baby. Would she, who was always so friendly, generous and hospitable to the Gypsies, be the child's godmother?

Christmas 1934 was a particularly special feast for Anna Maria Duysens.

On the morning of 24th December, in the Romanesque church of St. Catherina in Buchten, which had been decorated for Midnight Mass, the doctor's wife stood holding a child who was about to be christened. Once Pastor Jacobs had poured holy water over the baby, the child's names were entered in the baptismal register, and afterwards in the Register of Births and Deaths of the neighbouring department of Born, with the first two forenames that her godmother herself had received at her own christening: Anna Maria.

Anna Maria Steinbach, the Limburg Gypsy girl also known as Settela, would only live until she was ten.

Chapter 1

"74 Pers"

I must have seen the image of the girl in the door opening of the goods wagon — moving or paused and enlarged — at least forty or fifty times during the nineteen sixties, seventies, eighties and nineties.

In almost every television documentary about the Holocaust, her frightened face looks out of the wagon for a couple of seconds. Her photograph has been displayed in the section about the deportations and mass murder in most of the exhibitions of the years between 1940-1945 — a "still" from the film — showing the girl and the letters "74 Pers", chalked on the wagon in which she was taken away.

Every time I saw her picture, I asked myself who she was, what she was called — or what she had been called — because she might well now be dead. Where had she come from, this girl with the headcloth, how old had she been when someone in Westerbork pointed a camera at her; to what dreadful fate was she being carried in the goods or cattle wagon? Had she been gassed or killed, or did she die, weakened and exhausted in a distant camp, like Anne Frank — because the face of such a child would always make you think of Anne Frank. And when did she die, if she really was dead?

In the spring and summer of 1992 I saw her image eleven times on three separate occasions over a period of five weeks. First in the Oorlogs-en Verzetsmuseum (War and Resistance Museum) in Overloon where I visited the new, partially underground pavilion dedicated to concentration camps and the persecution of Jews. There she was again; the girl with the frightened gaze looked out at the exhibition hall from a photo panel more than one and a half metres high.

Two weeks later I was in the Herinneringscentrum Kamp Westerbork (Memorial Centre of Camp Westerbork) about which I had written a surly article for my newspaper at the beginning of the year. Plans had been proposed which had left me with the idea that the present impressive emptiness of the camp terrain was going to be disturbed by concrete reconstructions of the barracks which had previously stood there. But I realised later that I had misunderstood the plan, and when I walked round the area one lovely morning in June, I saw how tastefully the traces of the past had been restored to this bare field; it was no more than that. Later, in my newspaper, I fully and humbly acknowledged that I had misjudged the intentions of the management of the Westerbork Centre and had spoken out of turn.

That same June morning I visited the Exhibition Hall of the Remembrance Centre and watched an excerpt from the film which had been made in the then Juden Durchgangslager Westerbork (Westerbork Jewish Transit Camp). It was a compilation of pictures of industrial and everyday life in the factory barracks of Westerbork and the camp farm with its foals and lambs — then suddenly in sharp contrast, scenes of a train leaving for the east with deported camp inmates, an event which occurred almost weekly.

The film begins with old people sitting on the floor of a wagon, then there are pictures of a Jewish helper from the Ordnungsdienst (Camp Police) who is routinely closing a wagon door — then we see the seven second clip of the woodplanked side of the wagon pass by with "74 Pers" written on it, and the girl in the door opening.

Three weeks later, at the beginning of July, I was on holiday in Normandy. I watched a lot of French television in my rented appartment during the rainy and often overcast summer of 1992. One particular day the programmes dealt

9

mainly with one news item. This was the revelation that there were many highly qualified or prominent people in France who still remained unpunished despite their active involvement in a series of raids and the resulting handover of thirteen thousand French Jews to the Germans. This handover had taken place at the Paris Bicycling Sports Palace, known as Vélodrome d'Hiver, on the 15th and 16th of July 1942.

While the presenters reeled off their increasingly indignant *j'accuse* on the news slots of two o'clock, four o'clock, seven o'clock and eleven o'clock, an old black and white film of the Bicycle Palace in Paris was projected on the screen behind them, showing the group of Jews being rounded up with their bags and packs. To illustrate the deportation, the French producer used archive film from Westerbork, with its scenes of men and women boarding the train, and of course, the girl in the opening of the wagon door looked out into French living rooms for a few seconds.

I saw her four times on TF1 and five times on Antenne 2 that day. During a forum discussion about the scandal "Vélo d'Hiv" on Antenne 2 late that night, an enlarged shot of the girl served as a heartbreaking illustration of the matter the panel members were discussing so deeply and eloquently.

In December 1992 I heard that a few years earlier, the Remembrance Centre of Camp Westerbork had given a photo of the girl in the opening of the wagon door to twelve artists living in Drente. The artists were to take inspiration from this photograph and create "retrospective pictures" for a special exhibition.

When I later got hold of the catalogue of the 1990 exhibition, I read in the introductory notes that the girl "... is the personification of over 100,000 deported Jews. Rounded up in Camp Westerbork and from there to be *abgeschoben,* expelled. In a single journey to the east. Only a few thousand were known to have returned. Did the girl in the photo belong to the group of survivors? We do not know."

I took the two volumes of Jacques Presser's literary and historical tribute *Ondergang* (Downfall) — from my bookcase. Had Presser known something about the girl? It was some time since I had read his masterly account, subtitled, *De vervolging en verdelging van het Nederlandse Jodendom* (The persecution and extermination of Dutch Jewry). Perhaps the girl in the wagon was mentioned on one of the pages I had skimmed over or skipped due to the thickness of the chronicle.

I found her on page 291 of Volume Two. Here Presser described the film about Westerbork camp life, made at the behest of camp commandant SS Obersturmführer Albert Konrad Gemmeker, as "an irreplaceable, unique illustrated document." Presser writes that "... one excerpt has been shown all over the world, and is incorporated in every important film about National Socialism, and particularly about concentration camps, featuring, for example, in the French *Nuit et Brouillard*. It is a section from the excerpt *Eingang und Abfahrt* (Arrival and Departure), which was also shown, by the way, at Gemmeker's trial. I find it incomprehensible that Gemmeker did not suspect what a terrible indictment the film was, both of himself and of the system he served. Whoever sees this little girl, this helpless Jewish child, standing in mortal fear before the doors are closed, peering through a crack in the cattle wagon, wondering what kind of people are carrying her away to her unknown destination, will ask the same question."

Presser evidently didn't know who the young girl was either, the helpless Jewish child in this world famous film excerpt.

It was on that December afternoon in 1992, after I had put aside Presser's *Ondergang*, that I decided to search for the name of the young girl no matter how long it took, and find out what had happened to her after the *Ordnungsdienst* helpers on the Westerbork platform had bolted the wagon doors and the train had left the camp.

Chapter 2

A camp on the Drente heath

At the beginning of February 1993 I phoned Albert Gilbert, the Press Officer of the Herinneringscentrum Kamp Westerbork (Camp Westerbork Memorial Centre).

"No," he said, a little surprised by my question, "at least, as far as I know, there's never been any research done; perhaps the idea has come into someone's head, but it couldn't have led to anything, otherwise we'd know about it."

I had asked whether anyone had done any research about the girl. In the past week I had worked through lots of books about the Westerbork camp, but they hadn't provided me with a starting point. It had become clear to me that it was only through the film that I would find the trail of this girl; I needed to find out how the film had been made, by whom and when.

I asked Gilbert whether someone else had looked into the history of the Westerbork film. "No," he replied, "curiously not, you know. We obviously know a little about the film, but a proper study... That would be very rewarding, truly."

Gilbert invited me to come to Westerbork again.

I made an appointment at once. Then I set up a storage area in my personal computer, a "directory", in which I would keep all the results of my investigations. The computer asked me to type in a name. I decided to call my new directory, "Esther", because I considered that to be a beautiful name for a Jewish girl.

On 8th February, a cold, misty day, Gilbert, the Press Officer of the Camp Westerbork Remembrance Centre, took me round the former Durchgangslager in his car. We

12

drove through a forest, past the wooden villa where Camp Commander Gemmeker had lived from January 1943 till the middle of April 1945 with his mistress, Elisabeth Helena Hassel. (For several years a mysterious old lady had been granted permission to live in the villa, for reasons which nobody knew. Many people wanted to ask her if the spirit of the SS Obersturmführer still haunted the house in the woods near the barrier, but she never talked to anyone.)

Thin, spindly, winter-bare trees stood on the camp terrain, with bushes here and there; on the right a row of twelve tall radiotelescopes belonging to the Dwingeloo Observatory stretched into the sky. Workers were pottering about in the distance; they were, according to Gilbert, on their way from the back of the camp to lay fresh sods next to the train buffer, the spot where the old tracks had previously come to an end. In 1971 the artist Ralph Prins from The Hague had created a national monument here; two railtracks which rose on high in a sorrowful curve.

Gilbert had brought me here to show me the recently added educational museum and the camp terrain. Slopes half a metre high now mark the site where barracks had stood, and where the *Rampe* had been, the unpaved platform where the train had waited, aptly named by the inmates, *Boulevard des Misères* (Boulevard of Sorrow). A double barbed wire fence had been erected and I saw a few ruin-like constructions where the three punishment blocks 65, 66 and 67 had stood. Anne Frank had been imprisoned in barrack 67 from 8th August until 3rd September 1944.

"We've tried to recreate everything as authentically as possible," said Gilbert as we walked over a path strewn with crushed shells to the reconstructed part of a barrack wall. "Last week an old prisoner called Bob Cahen came here and said that the atmosphere was exactly as it had been — including the winter weather."

Not until 1982, thirty-eight years after the last train had left for the concentration and extermination camps in

Germany and Poland, was it suggested that this lonely spot in the forest of Westerbork should be turned into a National Memorial.

From 1939 to the early spring of 1945, the barracks which had stood on this plain on the heath of the sparsely populated province of Drente had been occupied by Jewish refugees from Germany. After 1st July 1942 however, when the Befehlshaber der Sicherheitspolizei und SD (Commander of the Security Police and SD), took over the Central Refugee camp of Westerbork as a Polizeiliches Juden Durchgangslager (Police Jewish Transit Camp), nearly all Dutch Jews were assembled here by the German occupiers. They were sent letters summoning them to assembly points near railway stations in major Dutch cities, or were taken from their houses or overpowered in raids and then transported to Westerbork.

Once in the Westerbork camp, they found a regime that was not so much controlled by the SS men as by the *alte Kampinsassen* (the German Jewish camp veterans who had been living there since 1939). Apart from the SS commandant, the Jewish Oberdienstleiter Kurt Schlesinger was the most powerful man in Camp Westerbork. Thanks to the outstanding Jewish organisation, minimal German input was needed to achieve the aim of the camp, the deportation of Jews to the work camps in Germany and Poland.

"What would otherwise have required dozens, if not hundreds of German soldiers and policemen to put into effect, was delivered ready made into the hands of the SS," Presser wrote in *Ondergang*. "For the Jewish inmates this was a terrible means of saving themselves, terrible because as a result of constant application, their task would have to degenerate into an objective in itself, acquiring the character of a task executed with precision and dedication."

The camp on the heath measured roughly five hundred square metres and was surrounded by barbed wire. The Germans named it after the nearest village in the area —

14

Westerbork; Lager Westerbork (Camp Westerbork). Westerbork was a transit camp for prisoners waiting to be sent to the places of the *Endlösung der Judenfrage* (Final Solution of the Jewish Question) — namely for extermination. In 1942, 1943 and 1944, 93 trains carrying over 101,000 Jews and 245 Gypsies left the unpaved platform of the camp. Following a two or three day train journey, 92,693 of them ended up in Auschwitz and Sobibor; the rest went to Theresienstadt and Bergen-Belsen.

The transports began on 15th July 1942; until the end of that year there were two or three trains a week. Initially the Jews had to walk about three kilometres from the camp to the little station of the village of Hooghalen, but in November 1942 the branch line leading into the camp was completed; the sleepers and rails were laid by the prisoners themselves under the supervision of the Nederlandse Spoorwegen (Dutch Railways).

Throughout the summer of 1943, a weekly train went back and forth from the camp, mostly on Tuesdays. During the rest of that year, three groups of deportees were taken away by train. In 1944, seventeen trains travelled from Westerbork to the concentration camps. The largest transport was on one of the nineteen trains for Sobibor; on June 8th 1943, 3,017 people were sent there from Westerbork.

The last train from Westerbork left on 13th September 1944 taking 279 people to Bergen-Belsen — or "Celle", as it was officially called, after the name of the medium-sized town in the area.

Of the 101,000 Jews deported from Westerbork, only 4,913 were still alive after the liberation; it is thought that about 40 of the 245 Gypsies survived.

On 12th April 1945, Camp Westerbork was liberated by Canadian soldiers. A small group of Jews who had escaped deportation continued living in the barracks for a few months longer. One part of the camp was now used for the internment of known members of the NSB (National-

Socialist Movement of The Netherlands), or those who had collaborated with the occupiers in other ways.

Just before 1950, after the prisoners had served their sentences, the camp stood empty. Then it became a refuge for Indian soldiers and their families from the KNIL (Koninklijk Nederlands-Indisch Leger — Royal Dutch-Indian Army) who felt unsafe in the new Republic of Indonesia. When they too left Westerbork, soldiers and their families from the former Dutch South Moluccan islands lived in the barracks. The camp was renamed Schattenberg, as some found the name Westerbork had a sinister ring. The last Moluccan family left the camp in 1969.

Two years later the barracks were broken up and low brushwood began to reclaim the rectangle of heathland. All traces of Jewish history faded from the plain, despite the unveiling in 1971 by Queen Juliana of the heart wrenching monument of the buffer with its abruptly foreshortened rails.

In 1981, the Dutch Communist Member of Parliament Joop Wolff drew the government's attention to the fact that a tragic but unforgettable part of the nation's heritage was being overlooked in Drente. Wolff's motion led to the opening of the Herinneringscentrum Kamp Westerbork in 1983, the Memorial Centre now visited annually by over one hundred thousand people, including many schoolchildren.

About 102,000 pebbles have been piled on the former roll-call area, one for every victim of Westerbork. While most of the stones bear a Star of David, 245 stones carry the picture of a flame. These flames represent the Gypsies who were sent from Westerbork to Auschwitz.

In the large hall of the Remembrance Centre where the computer monitors stand, Gilbert and I looked at the ten minute montage which had been compiled using scenes from the Westerbork film. The scenes are accompanied by a commentary from the camp diary of the Amsterdam journalist Philip Mechanicus. In the film, people are shown working in the forge, the keymaking workshop, the battery scrapyard, the shoe makers, the laundry; wagons are being wheeled over a narrow track, men lift parts of a barrack from a wide wagon, women sow the fields, the weather is lovely and it looks like autumn.

I saw pictures of Westerbork's leisure activities; a football match, a stage play, and cabaret artistes singing and dancing on the stage of the great hall.

Then a passenger train appears on the small screen; people disembark wearing the Star of David on their neat and wellmade clothes. A minute later another train arrives in the camp, this time an engine with goods wagons from which men wearing clogs get out, caps on their shaven heads. These are Jewish prisoners on punishment being sent to Westerbork from Vught concentration camp in the southern province of Brabant. From Westerbork they were transported to camps in Eastern Europe.

Now a third train; the camera lingers on this the longest, giving a comprehensive pictorial account of the routine preparations made for the departure of the weekly deportation train. People stand on the platform, waiting their turn to get in, and camp commander Gemmeker walks unhurriedly alongside the train, accompanied by his little dog and a couple of non-commisioned officers. There are young men and women with FK armbands. FK is short for Fliegende Kolonne (Flying Column), a task force made up of Jewish auxiliaries who assisted diligently on the platform. A man from the FK pushes a primitive stretcher bearing an old woman to the right and then to the left, further up, a man parts from a helper with a farewell handshake; a trolley with provisions for the journey is being unloaded; we see sausages and packets of the then popular Zeeuws Meisje margarine; in one wagon old people sit on the floor, leaning against sacks of straw.

And then there is the girl. The seven seconds, during which the camera moves from the side of the wagon with its chalked letters "74 Pers" to the crack in which the child stands and looks out, don't seem to belong to the film; they appear to be out of place, introduced suddenly into the otherwise fairly logical sequence of this part of the film with the scenes which make up *Eingang und Abfahrt*.

"What we know about the film," Dirk Mulder, the tall, fairhaired, forty-year old director of the Westerbork Memorial Centre told me that afternoon, "is that it was made in 1944 under the direction of Rudolf Breslauer, a Jewish photographer from Germany. Our document department gave us a few photocopies of correspondence from 1944 relating to the making of the film. But I think that most of the material can be found in the Rijksinstituut voor Oorlogsdocumentatie (State Institute for War Documentation) in Amsterdam."

As I left Westerbork that day I set myself a seemingly simple task.

First, I told myself, I would determine the date of the filming of the departing train. Then I would have to find out from the Oorlogsdocumentatie how many people had left Westerbork on that day in 1944 — it had to be between six hundred and a thousand. I needed to see the transport list of that day — which they must still have at the Rijksinstituut — and strike out the names of all the men, and all the women over sixteen or seventeen, because the girl did not seem to be older than that. That would probably leave fifty or sixty names.

One of those names would belong to the girl in the door opening. On the way home it occurred to me that she was actually the only child in the film. At first it struck me that this might simplify the search. Later I realised with horror that if the seven seconds were from another film, then these shots had been taken of another train on a completely different day. And someone, the film-maker Bresslauer or one of his assistants, or perhaps someone else making a montage after the war, had stuck that shot amongst the others, because, in Presser's words, of the "terrible accusation" it contains.

Could this be possible?

18

Chapter 3

Vorschläge für einen Film über Lager Westerbork (Proposals for a film about Camp Westerbork)

In February 1942, thirty-seven year old Rudolf Werner Breslauer was taken, with his wife Bella Weissman and their three children, from his home in Utrecht to the Westerbork camp. Breslauer had settled in Holland in 1938 after having been forced to leave his native Munich by the German anti-Jewish measures.

In Munich Breslauer had trained as an art photographer and printer, and with these skills found work in Holland as a lithographer, first with a printer in Leiden, then in 1941, with the Boekhoven publishing house in Utrecht.

Like many Germans of that time, Gemmeker, appointed as the new Westerbork camp commander in October 1942, was very interested in photography. This interest procured Breslauer a relatively comfortable position within the camp organisation, because Gemmeker put him in charge of supervising the photography department. The SS-Obersturmführer ordered a well equipped dark room to be set up for Breslauer in an upper space of the great hall of the camp. Here, Breslauer and his colleagues took identity photos of the prisoners, and also photographed all the various departments of the camp and the work performed there. In addition, Gemmeker and his girlfriend posed for sittings from which Breslauer meticulously produced beautiful salon portraits.

At the beginning of 1944, it was suggested that apart from taking photos of the camp, Breslauer should be allowed to record life in Westerbork on film. It is not clear

19

if camp commander Gemmeker first came up with the idea of Breslauer shooting a film or if his colleagues thought of it. In the latter case, Gemmeker would have agreed to the suggestion without hesitation. A film which showed how effectively and exemplarily the concept of *Arbeit macht Frei* (Freedom through Work) was being put into practice by the prisoners in Gemmeker's camp in the far north of Holland, would give his superiors in The Hague and Berlin reasonable grounds to officially denote Westerbork as an *Industrielager* (Industrial camp).

The importance of the camp and its commander could have saved the thirty-six year old Gemmeker from having to serve on one of the European fronts like so many other SS officers of his rank and age, where things were going so badly for Germany in the fifth year of the war.

In a small room in the seventeenth century Amsterdam mansion on the Herengracht, which has housed the Rijksinstituut voor Oorlogsdocumentatie since 1946, a file was set on the table before me. It contained letters and memos sent from Westerbork to the outside world from 7th March to 10th May 1944. All the correspondence was about the film.

After spending the whole morning and part of the afternoon reading all the correspondence, I felt dizzy. Every sentence was a desperate denial of the reality of camp life. I found no word or hint of what had gone on there, how people came to be there, or how the camp was run; the registration, persecution, raids, the bringing in and imprisonment of people in a camp on the heath, the trains which weekly transported a thousand inmates to the *Arbeitseinsatz* (Work camps) in the east. From the beginning of 1944, more than 90,000 men, women and children had been deported from Westerbork, and nothing more was ever heard of them, nothing. Before me lay the correspondence of members of an apparently normal society, in which life seemed to be led at a quiet pace and where sometimes, but only when absolutely necessary, a little more haste was demanded in the most friendly polite fashion.

I learned meanwhile that anyone who had a job in Westerbork clung on to it as if his life depended on it, because that was literally the case. The name of that worker would probably be left off the list of inmates drawn up on Monday evenings. That was the list containing the names of those who had to report for deportation on the Tuesday train.

It was the survival instinct that kept the members of the DB (Dienstbereich) 4, Gruppe 8, Fotografen (Department 4, Group 8, Photographs) constantly busy with their preparations for making their film in the spring of 1944. Rudolf Breslauer, apparently working with Heinz Todtmann, a Jewish *Dienstleiter* (Department Chief) and adjudant of the camp commander, drafted the layout of the film for Gemmeker on two sheets of A4 paper. *Vorschläge für einen Film über Lager Westerbork* (Proposals for a film about Camp Westerbork).

Breslauer stated the following in his synopsis (I translate the German text): "The film begins with a picture of a moving goods wagon turning off the main track. At the fork in the road there is a signpost with the inscription Lager Westerbork (Camp Westerbork). The shot dissolves into (*blendet über*) the Orange Canal where a ship cruises past a signpost (*Landestelle*). This signpost also points to Lager Westerbork. Dissolve to the country track Hooghalen-Rolde. A moving freight lorry turns off the road after a few metres to travel to Lager Westerbork. At this turning, again a signpost 'Lager Westerbork'. The freight lorry comes to a barrier. Stop. Control. The driver hands a piece of paper to the Military Policeman on duty. Close-up of the paper; we see the permit to enter the camp, written on the *Befehlshaber's* (Commander's) stationery, signed by the *Obersturmführer*. Close-up of the signature. Wide shot. The paper lies on the *Lagerkommandant's* office desk. Shot of *Obersturmführer*, photo of the Führer, etc. The *Obersturmführer* stands up, pulls on his coat and leaves the *Lagerkommandantur* (Camp command centre) to go out into the camp. Shot of the *Lagerkommandatur*."

Breslauer wanted the following part of the film to be a tour of the old camp, with pictures of the family barracks, camp activities, main kitchen, boiler house, bath house and hospital.

"The camp commander walks with visitors or supervisors around all the activities and remains in the Statistics Department for a while, where with the help of a chart of statistics and schedules (*Trickaufnahmnen*!) [trick shots] a short history of the camp is given: in the past it was a Dutch Government refugee centre for German Jews; the camp was taken over by the SD in July 1942."

Then, according to Breslauer's "Vorschläge", shots would be taken "of outgoing transports leaving for the Arbeitzeinsatz in the east, and then to Vught, Theresienstadt, Bergen-Belsen, Vitelles, and so on." Between brackets and question marks he suggested, "Pictures of incoming and outgoing transports, registration in the great hall, the bustle of people being put on the train, the closing of doors by the Ordedienst (OD-Absperrung), the Fliegende Kolonne (FK), the transport of the sick?"

Following these tentative suggestions for the synopsis, Breslauer continued with scenes he must have known would meet with Gemmeker's approval: "Wide shots over the high street in the direction of the new camp. The large barracks, the industrial activities, the work with all its bustle and variety. The camp as it is now, shown with all its activities; work places, industrial sector, work outside the camp, farm. The lives of the camp inmates; work, housing, recreation?

Dissolve to the camp commandant's study. Discussion at a round table with statistics of present production figures. Fade in; tour of inspection by the Lagerkommandant through the camp at night. Fade out. Night with a full moon. The silhouette of the camp with a huge chimney reaching to the night sky."

22

In the file about the Westerbork film compiled by the Rijksinstituut for War Documentation, I found eight sheets of paper which could be taken to be an editing plan, indicating how the pieces of film that had evidently already been shot and sent back to the camp after development should be cut and edited, and which text should be added where.

Part of the editing dealt with the farm and market garden of the inmates. In the column *Bild* (Pictures) the opening scene was described. "A flowering branch stretches towards the clouds, ploughs, digging," and in the column *Text*, "80,000 square metres of land, tilled by inmates, ensuring the camp will have food."

Next to the *Bild* of the Orange Canal stands the *Text*; "A waterway running alongside a road and a railway also connects the camp with the outside world..." Amongst pictures of the farm are shots of free-range chickens and hens, accompanied by the words "in camp Westerbork nothing is ever wasted (*kommt nichts um*). Kitchen waste is converted into eggs and fat. Director of the factory — Mother Nature." A shot of a sheep and a colt; *Text*; "Our youngest, May 1944 vintage!!!"

Two separate sheets show the editing scheme of that part of the film in which I was so interested, because there, in the final version, were the seven seconds with the girl in the door opening.

Breslauer or a colleague had given this a Main Caption; the preceding pastoral and industrial scenes only had an *undertitel* (caption).

The Main Caption read "Transport........." — I counted them. There were ten ominous dots. I give this part of the plan in its entirety, translated from German, first the shots, then, in quotation marks, the text which should link the film shots.

> Arrival of the train; 'Since July 1942, for almost two years, every time the same picture; Transport.'
> Transport handling details; 'This transport, from

Amsterdam, is a small, round hundred-and-twenty passenger type.'

OD near the train: 'The *Ordedienst* (Task Force) forms a cordon, helps the people getting out of the train, lines them up, counts them and leads them into the Registration area.'

Two young women from the FK carry a child's cradle; 'FK, Fliegende Kolonne, the organisation which assists at transports and also provides girls for all purposes.'

Transport from Vught; 'This time a goods wagon from KL Herzogenbusch.' (official SS name of the Vught concentration camp.)

Processing the transport in the great hall; 'Large transports are dealt with by the *Registratur* in the great hall. There are many people queueing. A shot of the long table.'

A separate shot of the registration: 'The card index being filled in. The distribution of camp cards. All food cards, rations, and so on, are given out and supervised by the CDK.'

There were another two pages belonging to the film section *Bunter Abend* (Variety Show) with the pile of papers from the *montageschema*. This part also had a Main Caption; 'Recreation.' These were shots which had been or might be taken of artistes imprisoned in Westerbork, who had appeared and triumphed in famous theatres, mainly in Berlin, over the last ten years.

Breslauer introduced the text accompanying the pictures of Willy Rosen, Erich Ziegler, Esther Philipse, Jetty Cantor, Lisl Frank and Otto Aurich singing, playing and performing revue sketches on the stage in the great hall, with the note, "Many of these once famous revue artistes give the camp dwellers a few happy hours after the day's work has ended."

Chapter 4

Die neue Schmalfilmschule
("The new 8mm-film school")

I could not find out when camp commander Gemmeker gave Rudolf Breslauer permission to start making the film, or whether he exercised any influence over the script. The first shots were probably filmed in March 1944. Breslauer was helped by Karl Jordan, a forty-year old Jew who had fled to Holland from Dortmund in Germany, settled in Hilversum, and had been taken to Westerbork on 13th February, 1942.

As I went through the pile of letters at the Rijksinstituut voor Oorlogsdocumentatie, I came across the names of others involved in the production of the film — camp commander Gemmeker, Abraham Hammelburg, W. Kloot, J. Eckmann, H. Hanauer and W. Heynemann.

The last three were members of the Contact-Afdeling (Contact-Department) in Amsterdam, a sort of last Jewish outpost in the capital.

The first letter I read had been written in Lager Westerbork on 7th March 1944 by Hammelburg to Eckmann and Hanauer in Amsterdam. Attached to the letter was a long questionnaire about a Victor film camera and a number of accessories.

Hammelburg wanted to know what the division in the viewer was in relation to the three object-lenses — whether the delivered spools of film would be daylight film spools and how they should be stored, how strong the light should be when a wide angle was used, and he also wanted a complete description of the Victor camera — "from its last owner." He required a splicer for sixteen millimeter film, and asked for a copy of the book, *Die neue Schmalfilmschule* (The new 8mm-film school).

The Contact-Department replied to this letter by phone. In a record of a "Telephone message from Amsterdam dated 15.3.1944," Hammelburg was informed that the view-finder mentioned was for a normal lens and the central image in the little window acted as a focus for the telephoto lens. Unfortunately, instructions for use of a Victor camera were not available, but the book, *Die neue Schmalfilmschule* would follow as soon as possible.

Hammelburg was asked to inform the Contact-Department which make of camera he preferred, Paillard or Howel? The following items were being sent to the camp by courier; "Book *Das Filmen ist schön* (Filming is beautiful), a splicer, 2 sets of film kit, 1 bottle acetone, 10 spools."

On 15th March, Hammelburg wrote to the Contact-Department again. From his letter it can be deduced that the preparations for the filming in Westerbork were in full swing. He wanted to exchange the reversible film for negative film of the highest possible sensitivity, and said that without this exchange another three hundred metres of film would be needed: "as the film has to last an hour, double the length of the necessary negative film must be calculated. All film, as long as the price is not too high, to be at the expense of Lager Westerbork."

Hammelburg adds: "Concerning the camera you supplied, it is quite ancient and the lenses clearly do not belong to it. So that our work can be carried out properly, a wellknown make of camera should be sent as a replacement. As the people concerned must start their work soon we request that you find another one as quickly as possible."

In response to another phone call between Westerbork and Amsterdam on 16th March, Hammelburg wrote saying that they would prefer a Siemens camera in the camp, but if nothing else was available, a Paillard would be acceptable. As the requested negative film was unobtainable, would Amsterdam please send six rolls of reversible film, each of one hundred and twenty metres.

Evidently everything went to plan; on 27th March 1944, "D.B. 5, Group 8, Photographs", reported the following to camp commandant Gemmeker;

"On 26 III. 1944 I received the following items from Mr Heynemann:
1. Siemens camera, with Meyer Optic, fl: 1.5 with grey filter in a leather bag.
2. 4 cassettes for each 15 metre film (more to follow).
3. 1 tripod.
4. 1 Bauer-Pantalux projector with Meyer Optik 1, 6 and 3 spools of each for every 120 metres, of which 2 spools are simple wire spoolers.
5. 1 titling apparatus "Atlas", incomplete (missing parts must be supplied).
6. 480 metre negative film 15/10 Din, Agfa FF Panchromatic.
7. 2 lightbulbs for title apparatus.
8. 1 small oil can, reserve capsules and a brochure.

The following items were returned to Mr Eckmann;
1. Victor-shot apparatus camera with 3 lenses.
2. Agfa projector.
3. 1 book letters, 1 title box, 1 resister.
4. The light metre is returned as the new one that was delivered is better.

On 29th March 1944, Rudolf Breslauer became involved in the correspondence. From barrack 14D he typed a letter to J. van der Zanden, director of Foto-en Cinehandel "Lux" in Breestraat, Leiden;

"It is precisely a year since I saw you in Leiden. Since then, according to what I have read in the papers, there has been a fire at the firm of Koningsveld. Has the company been able to continue working since the fire? When you speak to Mr Koningsveld, please say hello to him from me and give him my regards. Now, I have a request. Would it be possible for you to exchange two 8 and 9.5mm cameras for a good 16mm camera? If possible, of course, with a few cassettes...

Many thanks in advance for your trouble, with heartfelt greetings."

On 5th April, J. van der Zanden wrote to Breslauer, saying that he had been pleased to receive a sign that he was still alive. But unfortunately, it was not possible to effect Breslauer's proposed exchange. "A good 16mm camera is not available. Furthermore, it is completely impossible to deliver any film for it, because there are no stocks of this item and it is impossible to acquire any more."

Van der Zanden could not supply anything to the Westerbork film makers, or perhaps wanted no part in the dubious film production he may have suspected was taking place in Drente. Gemmeker himself wrote a courteous letter on 8th April, asking about a viewer for the editing of 16mm films. "A similar model stood in Gijtenbeek's shop window for some time; as you don't have one, could you perhaps get one from there." Van der Zanden replied on 13th April, "In answer to your letter I deeply regret that it will be impossible to send you the desired viewer. We have been in touch with the firm, but the aforementioned gentleman can absolutely not remember the last time a similar piece of apparatus was in his window. Presumably you mean the Odiscope which was on display, equipment for looking at small pictures, which anyway would not be suitable for your purposes."

On 12th April Gemmeker ordered some Philips-Arga lamps from Zeiss-Ikon in Amsterdam and on the same day sent a letter to the Gevaert enterprise in The Hague, explaining that he urgently needed ten dozen plates measuring nine by twelve cm for *Strichaufnahmen*.

Meanwhile Breslauer had apparently started working on the film, because on 14th April W. Kloot sent three boxes containing ninety-five metres of sixteen mm film, "with exterior shots", to Agfa in Arnhem. In the accompanying correspondence, Kloot complained about the quality of the developed film received from Arnhem the previous day, as the lighting was of an unsatisfactory quality. He suggested that a better result might have been achieved with a shorter development time.

At Agfa, the complaint from Westerbork was taken very seriously. In a letter dated 20th April, it was suggested that the mediocre quality might have been caused by an error in composing the shot. "If you disperse more light, for which you will obviously need another lamp, the result will be decidedly better," reads the implied criticism.

Chapter 5

A girl from the Fliegende Kolonne

From the montage scheme and the correspondence, I established that Breslauer had filmed in the months of April and May and perhaps also in the March of 1944. So it was clear that the train with the girl I was looking for had left Westerbork during this period.

In March, April and May 1944, the train entered the camp five times to take people away. On 3rd March 732 people went to Auschwitz, on 15th March the train took 210 people to Bergen-Belsen and on 23rd March it transported 599 people to Auschwitz.

On 5th April the engine drew three wagon units out of Westerbork; one with 289 people going to Theresienstadt, one with 240 people for Auschwitz. A third unit transported 101 people to Bergen-Belsen.

On 19th May the train from Westerbork comprised of two wagon units; one took 238 people to Bergen-Belsen, the other took 453 peple to Auschwitz.

At which departure had Breslauer been present with his film camera?

After leaving the Rijksinstituut voor Oorlogsdocumentatie having read through the correspondence about the film, I went to see René Kok. He was the manager of the Rijksinstituut's photo and film archives which were located in an annexe only a kilometer away down the Herengracht.

I had known René Kok for some years; he was in his mid-thirties and his boyish cheerfulness masked an encyclopaedic knowledge about the Occupation. I knew that news of my search would appeal to him — he himself had spent many years doing nothing else but researching the history of the many thousands of photos in his archives.

When I told him that I wanted to find out about the girl in the Westerbork film, his reaction was: "And it's about time too!"

Not that he thought he could give me much help. All he knew about the Westerbork film was that it had somehow popped up after the war and landed up in the Oorlogsdocumentatie. "I remember once reading a report which said how moved former colleagues at our Institute had been by the sight of what things were like in Westerbork. More than that, little is known about the film. It was shown at the trial of camp commander Gemmeker, and later at the trial of Rauter, the highest SS-policeman in the Netherlands."

René Kok took a tape of the Westerbork film and put it in the video player. Together we watched pictures of a train leaving Westerbork on the TV screen. Suddenly Kok shouted; "There, the girl walking there, she's still alive! Perhaps she knows something — why didn't I think of that before?"

He stopped the film at the shot of a group of young men and women who had just come onto the platform. Their armbands bearing the letters FK: Fliegende Kolonne, showed they were members of the team of helpers always present at the arrival and departure of the train.

"The one on the left is Mrs Cohen," said René Kok, "she survived Westerbork and another camp too. I have her address."

Ten minutes later I was speaking to a Jules Cohen on the telephone, the husband of the Lenie Nijstad who had been a member of the Fliegende Kolonne in Westerbork. Cohen had a low voice and a quiet manner. He didn't seem at all surprised by my request to visit him and his wife to talk about the Westerbork film.

"Yes, my wife appears in the film," he said. "I also have the film on video. The Rijksvoorlichtingsdienst (State Information Service) only let us have it because of our exceptional circumstances — our personal connection with

31

the film." Cohen made an appointment with me. He said he would wait for me next day in front of his house with a resident's parking card, as it was very difficult to park in his south Amsterdam neighbourhood. He also said: "May I ask how old you are, Mr Wagenaar?"

"I'm fifty-three."

"That's nice. Are you Jewish?"

"No, and as far as I know, I have no Jewish relatives."

"Oh, it doesn't matter. It's just that before the war there was a famous rabbi in Amsterdam called Wagenaar. Until Monday then."

René Kok promised to do his best to be present on Monday afternoon when I spoke with the Cohen couple.

Jules Cohen was a short stout man with an open face and a jovial appearance. As he welcomed me at the door of his basement flat, he asked again how old I was, and evidently found my age satisfactory. When we got inside the house he introduced his wife, Lenie Cohen-Nijstad, a small, well-groomed woman with grey hair. She seemed a bit short-tempered.

Now a pensioner, Cohen had been born in the north of Holland in 1921, the son of a corset maker. Lenie Nijstad was born in 1924. The two were married in the summer of 1943. They had been allowed to leave Westerbork and go to Amsterdam for their wedding but shortly after the ceremony the couple had to return to camp. Jules Cohen left Westerbork a few times after that; he was once sent to Arendsburg, in the Sperrgebiet of The Hague for a couple of days. There he had to hang wallpaper in a house commandeered by a German officer, situated near the empty international headquarters of Shell.

Lenie Cohen worked as a member of the Fliegende Kolonne in Westerbork from 29th September 1943 to 4th September 1944; she had kept the worksheets setting out her duties in connection with the train, work usually carried out on Tuesdays. On September 4th 1944 she herself was transported to Theresienstadt, together with her husband.

When I asked when Mrs Cohen might have been filmed as a member of the Fliegende Kolonne helping the people leaving from the platform, Jules Cohen stood up and went to fetch a scrapbook from an upper room.

When he sat down again and opened the album, he seemed cautious and reverent. A yellow Star of David had been pushed behind the plastic of the inner cover. Fascinated, I looked at the fragment of cloth. Cohen saw how interested I was and said, "Yes, the star belonged to me, I wore it."

He thumbed through the book, revealing snaps taken in Westerbork and scraps of worn yellowish paper. "That's camp money from Theresienstadt," said Cohen, "I have kept everything." A split pin had been stuck into one of the sheets of the album pages; a tool from Theresienstadt.

René Kok, an insatiable collector, visibly held his breath. Then he said; "Should there come a time when you don't know what to do with all of this, I'd be happy to take it all off your hands."

Cohen said that he would bear Kok in mind. Then he half apologised for the album. "We are mad to have kept everything — we are nuts. Lucky really, that we are nuts, otherwise we wouldn't still be on this earth!" He took the album back upstairs. In the course of the afternoon the book was consulted a few more times. Each time Jules Cohen brought the book down and took it back up again; he went up, he came down, it was like a ritual.

Mrs Cohen, who had started working with the train at the beginning of 1944, told me two dates she would never forget. "On 15th February of our last year in Westerbork, I accompanied my grandmother to the train, on 15th March I took my parents to the platform. People who reproach us for our work in the Fliegende Kolonne don't know what it was like in Westerbork. Had I refused to work, I'd have had to get into the train myself."

33

Jules Cohen took a couple of his wife's worksheets from the album, summonses for platform service dating from the last months of 1943. It seemed that Lenie Cohen-Nijstad should have been on train duty on 4th April 1944, but she did not appear on the *Rampe* (platform). She was ill with jaundice and was exempt from work until mid May. When she was better, she was sent as a member of the Fliegende Kolonne to work for a while in the nearby town of Assen, as a cleaner at the *Ortskommandatur* (German local command post) in Port Natal.

From the four worksheets we ascertained that Mrs Cohen had been on duty during the first few months of 1944, when the transport I was looking for had been filmed. She had definitely been present on 15th February and 15th March. There were no worksheets to prove she had been present at the transports of 25th February, 3rd March, 15th March and 23rd March 1944. On 4th April she had been ill, and was therefore not present at the transport of 5th April, and she was working in town until the middle of May.

There was no evidence that she had been present at the transport of 19th May 1944, because then, as far as she could remember, she had to work in Port Natal in Assen.

René Kok and I concluded that Mrs Cohen must have been filmed on 15th March. But that was impossible too; on 15th March a relatively small group of 210 people had been sent to Bergen-Belsen. We knew that third class coaches were always used for transports going to Bergen-Belsen. It was true that a couple of coaches could be seen in the Breslauer film, but the film actually focussed on the bustle near a long row of goods wagons.

Jules Cohen asked if we would like to see the film again. He still had the Rijksvoorlichtingsdienst copy on the Betamax 2000 videosystem — it was due to this ancient recording of the Westerbork film that the couple still hadn't bought a new video-recorder with a contemporary cassette system.

Mrs Cohen said: "I saw the Westerbork film on television on one of the 4th May Remembrance Days. I looked at it and thought: is that me or not? But a little later the telephone rang and someone said; "Do you know what? We've just seen you on TV." Some time after that my son rang from Israel; he'd also seen me in a television programme which had shown the film. Then we found out where we could get the film and the Rijksvoorlichtingsdienst got us a copy."

No, Lenie Cohen had never seen a film of the transports being made in Westerbork. "You were always so busy working with the train," she said. "There were people asking if I could buy something for them, or if I could notify a relative, or there might be someone who didn't have any soap. No one knew exactly what was going on, where they were going on the train. We didn't know either."

The film began; Lenie Cohen-Nijstad saw herself. "There, see those people standing next to the cart, I know them all," she said.

A young man with a white cap came into view — that was one of her brothers; he supervised the loading of barrels onto the train. As the train left the camp, a young man rode a little way on the engine. The Cohens recognised him: he was from Assen. "He brought the post for everyone, he was a good lad."

Jules and Lenie Cohen couldn't help us further. When Jules saw the picture of the girl at the wagon door, he mumbled, "Yes, she is world famous, that child. But I don't find it particularly strange that she's never been recognised."

He explained why before we left, giving us a picture of prewar Amsterdam Jewry, which had largely been made up of the working classes. "People were desperately poor, living in basements in wretched circumstances. There were streets in Amsterdam that were entirely Jewish, house after house. These people couldn't flee or hide from the Germans. Nor did they know who their enemy was.

35

None of them had ever harmed a fly, most of them had never been out of Amsterdam and in many cases hadn't ever left the Jewish quarter."

With this description Cohen tried to give us an idea of the anonymity of many of the people transported from Westerbork. They were a nameless mass which included that one girl. These almost nameless victims made up the majority of those departing on the train.

But, I objected, the girl only left Westerbork in the spring of 1944 — so she must have been 'spared' for a while. She and her family might have been on one of the famous "lists", and therefore temporarily exempt from the transports. If that was the case she was by definition not anonymous.

Jules Cohen saw that at once and began to doubt his own theory. Maybe the girl belonged to a family in hiding who had been picked up, he suggested, an S-case? (*Straf-case* — punishment case.) This would explain the girl's headcloth; the punished prisoners usually had their heads shaved before being taken to Westerbork. They had to wait for the transport in a special barrack surrounded by barbed wire: the S-sector. This *Straf* sector formed a camp within a camp.

But Mrs Cohen, who knew how the transports worked, said that prisoners were always pushed quite roughly into the wagons, and never had time to look calmly out of the crack of a wagon door.

The Cohens advised me to seek out survivors of the transports from spring 1944 — perhaps one of them would recognise the girl. But they didn't think I would have much luck.

At the door Jules Cohen asked for the third time about my age; he thought that I looked much younger than fifty-three. "That isn't an advantage when you come to ask our kind of people about the past. We're from a different time."

Chapter 6

An afternoon in a Scheveningen bunker

In The Hague district of Duindorp, at the end of tram line
12, a paved track leads into the dunes of Scheveningen. On
the map it is marked as Baden Powellweg, after the
British founder of the Scout Movement. In the 50s and
60s, before environmentalists protected this dune area,
there had been a clubhouse here which belonged to a
group of Cubs, Boy Scouts, and Rangers from The Hague,
who were able to play, roam freely, and light fires in the
dunes.

The winding lane divided at one point, and I continued
driving leftwards past a couple of sheds belonging to the
Parks and Recreation Body of Groenvoorziening Local
Authority. Then I came to a dead end in a sandpan full of
thick sticks and creepy looking tree roots. It was very quiet
and a little spooky.

I turned the car round and took the right hand fork,
which brought me to a building at the bottom of another
sand pan. This was a surprisingly modern-looking office
building which had been converted from a German
bunker, dating back to the time when the Scheveningen
wilderness was part of the Atlantic Wall. It was here that
the Photo and Film Archive of the Rijksvoorlichtings-
dients (State Information Service) had been established
nearly ten years ago.

I was welcomed by Ruud van der Kley, an educated man
wearing fragile glasses, who was in charge of most of the
historical films in the bunker. He explained that the former German fort had been chosen as a storage place
because it was made of reinforced concrete, and the nitrate
film which had been used before and just after the war,
was very flammable and produces oxygen. So should a fire
break out, it would be almost impossible to extinguish.

It was a Thursday afternoon, 18 March 1993. Five minutes after my arrival René Kok came in; he had made this
appointment for me with the Rijksvoorlichtingsdienst
and wanted to participate in the proceedings. After Kok
had heartily greeted Ruud van der Kley, whom he visited
regularly, he told me that Mrs Cohen had phoned him a
couple of days previously. Following our afternoon meeting, the Cohens had gone over our conversation and then
consulted a friend who had also been in the Fliegende
Kolonne at Westerbork. Mrs Cohen told her friend that
they had been visited by a man from The Hague who was
researching the identity of the famous child between the
wagon doors. After talking it over, Mrs Cohen and her
friend had been able to recall that in April or May 1944,
a "Gypsy transport" had left Westerbork. This was a
"combined" train taking people to Auschwitz, Celle, then
on to Bergen-Belsen, Theresienstadt and Ravensbrück.
"And your girl looks a little like a Gypsy," said René Kok
at the end of his story.

Yes, but also East European, a little Slavic, and also
shabby, and also Jewish — that didn't really help us at all.

Ruud van der Kley picked up the cannister containing
the film we had come to see. It held the four *aktes*
(scenes) he had pasted together from the spools of film he
had received in June 1986 from the Nederlands
Filmmuseum. For years the museum had kept these
excerpts in another coastal bunker, in Overveen, near
Haarlem. They were catalogued there under number
1077 t/m 1085, with the note; "... the most original material. (The film was probably shot on 16mm negative, but
no one has ever seen this material.)"

"I think we're about to do something very interesting,"
said Van der Kley. "Of course, I know the Westerbork film
quite well, but I've never really examined it properly." He
lay the first roll of film, roll — 2 — 1167 *Akte* 1 — on the
turntable of his well-appointed editing suite, and slowly for-
warded it on a few frames. He switched on the machine, and

on the glass screen I saw the sharp pictures of a train approaching camp Westerbork.

Van der Kley paused the shot. This was the first time he had looked intently at the Westerbork film and his skilled eyes had at once noticed a splice, a break line, where two pieces of film had been stuck together. He played the film back on the spool and ran his thumb and forefinger along it. The splice was in the film, he said, he could feel no unevenness on the celluloid. So, he concluded firmly, this film is not the original cinematographic Westerbork document, but a copy.

(Later René Kok himself would wonder aloud if the Film Museum had kept the original copy. If not — where was it? "I'll have to make some discreet enquiries at the Film Museum," Kok resolved.)

The train on the screen began to travel a little way, but Van der Kley stopped the film again. He had seen something else which Kok and I had missed; there was a small stamped impression discernible on a couple of the film shots. He took the film out of the spool and lay one section, frame by frame, under the inspection lamp on the table. When he had enlarged it, the writing on the seal became legible; "*Le Bourget, Douane Française.*"

"So at some time, this film has been to France," said Van der Kley.

René Kok rummaged through the papers he had brought with him. He agreed with Van der Kley's conclusion and showed us a letter dated 17 May 1949, in which Lou de Jong, then director of the Rijksinstituut voor Oorlogsdocumentatie, asked if the "Westerbork film with the footage of the transports" could be sent to the Centre de Documentation Juive Contemporain in Paris. Or, De Jong continued, if this was not possible, could a copy of the film be made — and what, roughly, would it cost? Another letter from the Oorlogsdocumentatie from the pile of papers on René Kok's lap said that the "outgoing transport" in the film was a "combined" transport on its way to Auschwitz and Celle.

We continued to watch the Westerbork film. *Akte* 1 contained the transport section. There was the train of third class coaches which had come from Amsterdam. The people who got out were wearing neat warm clothes; these were not day trippers, but proper travellers. Three Dutch Military Policemen came across the platform with two nurses. Then the train with prisoners from Vught; shaven headed, clogs, cold weather. After they had stepped down onto the platform, someone in the row was greeted by a man from the Jewish Ordnungsdienst who was walking along quickly. Somone in the front of the queue was slapping himself to keep warm.

Then part three of the transport scenes in the Westerbork film, the outgoing transport to "Auschwitz and Celle." People, ready and packed. It seemed as if they had just arrived at Westerbork, but no, it soon became clear that they were going on a journey out of the camp. We saw an old man with a pointed grey beard, dark jacket and scarf, at first he had no luggage, and then suddenly he was dragging a blanket roll and a box. I saw the old man three times. Behind him a man and woman embraced; farewell? Now a passenger train was visible with goods wagons behind it — or were they cattle wagons? Near a wagon on which the number 10 had been chalked, a helper came up pushing an old woman on a stretcher with extremely high wheels. He went past the wagon with the chalked number 9. There the stretcher bearer turned the strange cart around and walked back.

Shot of wagon with chalked number 12. There were provisions to take on board; packets of margarine and thick sausages. I watched unabashed and looked very intently inside one of the wagons. There on the floor sat a man wearing a hat, next to him, leaning against some straw bales, sat a woman. She brought a hanky to her face, as if to wipe her nose. A little later I saw her rub her eyes. Was she weeping? The following shot: Germans in uniform walking over a nearly empty platform. Gemmeker and his dog went by.

Then the seven seconds with the girl in the door opening started up. What was the number chalked on her wagon? Ruud van der Kley spooled the film pictures back and slowed them down again, letting them run so slowly that we could almost see the top and bottom line of each film frame on the screen. The number on the wagon might have been a 10; the 1 was clearly visible but one side of the 0 could have formed part of a 6. Next to the number was the infamous inscription "74 Pers", with its elegant and flamboyant "P".

The camera goes up to the left and along the gap in the wagon doors, and rests on the girl's face. Her eyes move and look past the camera. There is a small movement in her face; is it fear? Her small hand is holding something tightly, we cannot see what, it could be the handle of an umbrella or a walking stick.

The girl disappears from view. Wagons 8 and 9 are visible. A man from the Ordnungsdienst shuts the door of wagon 9 and fastens down the latch. On the platform there is a discussion between SS-officers who are standing around camp commandant Gemmeker. One of them signs a list which a man in civilian clothes is holding — prisoner, member of the Jewish camp leadership? Then we see the opposite side of the engine in a cloud of steam. The train begins to move, Germans holding rifles stand on the footplates, wagons pass by, we make out the numbers on their sides, 8, 9, 10...

Shocked, I cried out, "Stop!" It suddenly occurred to me that all the train wagons we had just seen passing, and those which had been standing at the platform earlier, had sides made from horizontal planks. But the side of the wagon in which the girl stood had <u>vertical</u> planks!

How could this be possible? It surely wasn't some trickery, that wagon with the lonely child in the door opening?

"This is the worst thing that could have happened to you," René Kok said earnestly, breaking the silence. He looked at me as if we had both been forced back to square one. So the seven seconds showing the girl were not from the transport filmed on that day by Breslauer, but from a completely different day — perhaps not even shot in Westerbork. In the past Kok and I had commented that the short scene was so isolated; nothing preceded and nothing followed it. One minute the girl was there and the next she was gone.

"After the war, the documentary film director Max de Haas staged a Jewish transport scene for a film about the *Knokploegen* (armed Resistance squads)," said René Kok, making matters worse. Hell and damnation, what now?

Ruud van der Kley, who had also been affected by our conclusion, started the film again and the long train continued its journey out of camp Westerbork. Look! Another wagon with vertical planks went past! We spooled the film right back to the bit where the long train was first seen passing the platform, and examined the wagons. And then we saw another two wagons with vertical wooden boards.

"The wagon with the girl in it really does belong to this train," René Kok announced with great relief.

We now let the train roll out of the camp very slowly and spooled forwards and backwards over part of a wagon with chalk marks on its right. Was that the "P" for Pers? It was clear that the side of the wagon was made from vertical planks; there was a small door section with a slight bulge on the righthand side. When we had seen these slow motion pictures about ten times, we agreed: it was the same wagon in which the girl had made her journey to Auschwitz in the spring of 1944.

We could now confirm the train's destination with an old note that René Kok produced from the Oorlogs-documentatie; "Departure, combined, transport to Celle and Auschwitz". To Celle — Bergen-Belsen — the journey is always made with passenger coaches; on the journey Westerbork-Auschwitz the engine always pulls goods or cattle wagons.

"Now you're getting somewhere," said René Kok.

But I realised that, in the course of that afternoon, I had still got no further to finding out the date when Breslauer filmed the train transporting prisoners from the Westerbork Jewish Transit Camp. And until I knew that date, I wouldn't know in which transport list to look for the girl's name.

As I left the bunker, Ruud van der Kley told me which official route I could take to try to get the Rijksvoorlichtingsdienst to send me a video copy of the Westerbork film. "The Rijksvoorlichtingsdienst isn't usually too generous," said Van der Kley. "But you've made a serious impression on me."

It had grown darker in the Scheveningen dunes; I had to switch on my headlights in order to drive back to the land of the living and find the pavement near the terminus of line 12 again.

Chapter 7

Wim Loeb, member of the *Gruppe Fotografen* (Photography Group)

In May 1990, the Dutch television channel TROS showed the film *Kamp van hoop en wanhoop* (Camp of Hope and Despair). Seventeen survivors of the Westerbork camp took part in this documentary made by Willy Lindwer. Their testimonies were later published in a book, interspersed with a historical overview of Camp Westerbork by the young historian Karin van Coeverden. She also gave a brief description of Rudolf Werner Breslauer, brief because little of note is known about the German photographer. Despite serving SS Obersturmführer Gemmeker so well, Breslauer, together with his family, was dispatched to Theresienstadt on the penultimate train from Westerbork on 4th September 1944. Breslauer was taken to Auschwitz on 24th October; his wife Bella Breslauer-Weissman and their three children followed two days later, by which time Rudolf Werner Breslauer was already dead, having been gassed immediately on arrival in Auschwitz. Of Breslauer's family, only one daughter, Ursula, survived the Holocaust.

On page 50 of *Kamp van hoop en wanhoop*, Breslauer is mentioned as the camp photographer, and I read: "A short time later, Breslauer was given an assistant, who had arrived in Westerbork in September 1942. Willem L. (Wim) Loeb, was also a photographer and helped with developing films and retouching the pictures... Wim Loeb, unlike Breslauer, stayed at Westerbork until the end of the war, apart from a short time in 1943. ... It was cameraman Breslauer who shot the 16mm film of seventy minutes duration, assisted by Wim Loeb, who also worked on the editing."

Was Wim Loeb still alive? If so, would he know when Breslauer had pointed his camera at the girl in the wagon door? I telephoned Karin von Coeverden in Diemen. "Yes," she said, "As far as I know, Mr Loeb is still alive. I think he lives in or near The Hague."

I found two Loebs in The Hague telephone book. One was not at home, the other answered the phone cheerfully with the name Loeb. When I asked if he knew a Wim Loeb who had been involved with photography during the Occupation whilst a prisoner in camp Westerbork, the man replied with a series of slight sighs which lasted for almost one minute. I too became short of breath at my own impudence as the silence from the other end of the line continued.

"You fling me rather unexpectedly back into a time which I don't want to think about any more," the man said finally. "I was not sent to Westerbork myself, but I am Jewish and have other vivid memories of those years."

He knew of no Loeb in his family who was or who had been a photographer. He gave me the telephone number of a relative who had been in Westerbork, a woman living in Voorschoten.

When this lady picked up the phone I spoke to her cautiously. I apologised for disturbing her, told her who I was, and explained that I had been given her phone number by one of her relatives in The Hague, who had told me that she had been sent to camp Westerbork for some time.

Without hesitation and in a friendly voice the woman said; "Yes, that was on the 4th or 5th September; I was twenty-one then, and they took me to Theresienstadt. I survived, as you can hear."

I explained I was researching the film that had been made by someone called Breslauer in the spring of 1944 in Westerbork. He had worked with a Wim Loeb. Did she know the latter, was he perhaps family?

"No," the woman replied. Nor could she remember a film ever having been made in Westerbork. But, sure, she knew there was a Westerbork film — she had seen the pictures more than once on television.

45

"You can see the toy workshop in the film," she said. "That's where I worked for quite a while. That workshop was the great passion of camp commandant Gemmeker; in my opinion it was his own idea to set it up. It's possible that we were filmed, though as far as I know, I'm not in the film. And I might have seen the filming, but I would have most likely kept out of the way."

Then, almost half a century after she had been in Westerbork, this woman gave me by telephone a lesson in camp survival. She taught me that the art of survival in a concentration camp boils down to this; look in front, look down, never look up or around.

"That Gemmeker, he must have come into our workshop at least fifty times. But when you ask me what he looked like, I must apologise for not being able to answer you — you never looked at a man like him, you'd only look at him as he was leaving, look at his back. In Westerbork, it was life threatening to make eye contact with a German, because then you lost your anonymity and they might ask you for your name. And that could mean that your card had been marked for the transport."

"You know," she continued. "I might have noticed, out of the corner of my eye, someone using a camera in Camp Westerbork. But I must have thought: Keep out of the way! Don't get involved with a film! There were probably always Germans from the SS around and then you had to keep out of the way. In Westerbork it was best to make yourself scarce when a train was leaving, because if Gemmeker was short of three passengers to make up his quota, there was always the possibility that you would have to get in."

She talked in the same vein for almost three quarters of an hour, interrupted now and then by my questions, and before we said goodbye, she said, "Do you know that I haven't talked about Westerbork in forty years? But my memories aren't buried as deeply as I imagined, and now I've noticed that, I've shocked myself a little."

46

Then she thought of something that might help me; she didn't know any Wim, but she knew of a Pim Loeb from Westerbork. "He was about ten years older than me and he took photographs. I think he became supervisor of the photo department at De Bijenkorf in Amsterdam after the war."

She looked for Pim's telephone number but could only come up with the number of his sister who lived in Prinsengracht in Amsterdam. Five minutes later the sister was telling me that Willem Loeb was still alive and had seemed to be OK and in good health the last time she had seen him.

Before she gave me her brother's telephone number, she asked me why I wanted it. "Because I'm researching into the film from Westerbork," I answered.

"*Ach,*" she said, "that's the film where the door closes on the tragic girl; I know what you mean. My brother lives in Rustenburgerlaan in Haarlem."

At the end of March 1993, Wim Loeb received me in his beautiful prewar house, situated in a Haarlem lane which must have been quiet and peaceful until being discovered as a short cut by urban drivers. Loeb was an unassuming, neatly dressed man with thin grey hair, who assessed me with his clever, friendly eyes. He had been getting a pension for ten years, accrued while working at the De Bijenkorf fancy goods department store. There Loeb had been responsible for the firm's assortment of photographic apparatus and clocks.

He was born in The Hague in 1916, the son of a Jewish gynaecologist who worked in a busy practice in this seat of Dutch government. In the thirties, Wim Loeb had studied graphic art and advertising, as well as photography, at The Hague Academy of Arts. This background ensured that when he was sent to Westerbork at the age of twenty-six, he was introduced into Rudolf Breslauer's *Gruppe Fotografen*, where Karl Jordan worked too.

47

Loeb sat me down on the couch in his study. His wife brought in tea and cakes and remained while we talked. She was about seventy, good-looking and bold, sometimes a little grumpy. In the course of our conversation, I became aware that the testiness and energy she exuded — particularly when stirred by her husband's memories — had apparently saved Loeb's life and had certainly alleviated his situation in Westerbork. As his non-Jewish wife, she had travelled regularly from Amsterdam to the Westerbork camp in Drente during the two periods Wim Loeb was imprisoned there, meeting her husband secretly behind the camp farm with packets of delicacies. Another reason for Mrs Loeb's sharp manner stems from the occasion her young husband was threatened with sterilisation in Westerbork.

(I read about Mrs Loeb's intervention in this matter when I reread Presser's work *Ondergang*, in which her name is mentioned. At the end of May 1943, Aus der Fünten, chief of the Security Police and SD in Amsterdam, and responsible for the deportation — *Auswanderung* — [Forced Emigration] — of Dutch Jews, went to Westerbork and in the great hall of the camp, addressed a group of prisoners who were in racially mixed marriages. They were given the choice of being sterilised or "...well, you all know what happens here every Tuesday" — the day of the deportation train. They had half an hour to decide — those who left the room would be considered to have refused sterilisation. Wim Loeb went out of the room and made clandestine contact with his young wife. Presser tells us, "She immediately rushed round to Zöpf's private house in her fear and rage [Zöpf was head of the Referat IV B 4 in The Hague]. Luckily for Mrs Loeb, Zöpf knew nothing or claimed to know nothing about Aus der Fünten's actions, and in response to his visitor's agitated reproaches, he telephoned at once and intervened. So the refusers just got off with a fright...")

Mrs Loeb told me that her husband had got his job as photographer in Westerbork thanks to her intervention with SS officer Zöpf. Wim Loeb agreed; his so-called "parachuting" into the photograph department because of Zöpf's recommendation had initially aroused Breslauer's mistrust. But Loeb quickly proved to be a good and hardworking member of the *Gruppe Fotografen*, and Breslauer's suspicions faded away.

"The job wasn't actually so hard," said Wim Loeb. "The main part of the work was making identity photos. The identity photos were needed for people on a specific list. Our work represented a sort of quasi hope. Don't imagine that we Westerbork photographers were a hardworking group constantly occupied with taking, developing and retouching photos. It was really the luxury hobby of commander Gemmeker, through which people were exempted from transportation and supposed to find freedom. Gemmeker was mad about photography.

"Our darkroom was in a cabin behind the film projector in the performance hall of the camp. I was able to look into the hall through a little shutter. I saw the symphony orchestra of Westerbork rehearsing a couple of times; there must have been almost half the Amsterdam Concertgebouworkest sitting there."

Then we got onto the subject of the Westerbork film. I had told Loeb over the telephone that I would bring the videocopy I had recently received from the Rijksvoorlichtingsdienst. Loeb had promised that he would prepare himself for this and rack his memory in the meantime. Now he said he was probably going to disappoint me; he had never done any filming in Westerbork himself. Nor had he ever assisted Breslauer in filming, despite what it said in the book I had told him about over the phone.

Wim Loeb could remember absolutely nothing about a "commissioned" film in which Breslauer and other members of the photograph group had been involved — and he

49

didn't have the faintest idea when the shots of the departing train had been filmed.

"By the way," he said, "I never went near the train; I kept as far away as I could. I had the superstitious feeling that as long as I never saw the train leave, I would never have to leave in it." Then he said something that surprised me; he had spent several days working on the film after Breslauer had already been taken from Westerbork. He had edited perhaps five thousand metres of developed film shots — and this astounded me even more — which resulted in two more or less complete films about Westerbork.

"My story begins after September 1944," Loeb related. "The camp was empty and quiet. The last train had left in mid-September and about seven hundred Jews remained in the camp. I was the only one left from the Photograph Department Group. I had to organise all the work and sort out the photographs myself. I did this in one of the houses of the *alte Kampinsassen*, the first refugees who had ended up in Westerbork; it was a sort of hut which had been built as a workplace. I slept there too. I buried some of the photos in a hole under the steel doormat of the house. When the camp was liberated, I dug them up, that was in April 1945. Later I gave a set of the photos to the Oorlogs-documentatie, to Mr De Jong."

While he had been clearing out and sorting the photographs, Loeb came upon cannisters or cans containing fragments of films. It was some time after September 1944 — he didn't know precisely when. There must have been about four to five thousand metres of film in each can. It was all eight millimeter cine film. Wim Loeb had already mentioned this over the phone when I first contacted him. He had said: "It was eight millimetre film, not sixteen, I've worked in photography long enough to know the difference between eight and sixteen millimetre cine film!"

I told him that it was certain that Breslauer had shot most of the film, if not all of it, with a sixteen millimeter

50

camera. This had been confirmed by the correspondence about the Westerbork film and also by Ruud van der Kley, the expert from the Rijksvoorlichtingsdienst. "That may well be," said Loeb, but he insisted a little obstinately: "What I had in my hand was eight millimeter wide film, there's no doubt about it!"

My respect for him, coupled with my reluctance to upset my benevolent witness with any further objections, stopped me from trying to correct what I considered to be his distorted recollections.

Amongst the film fragments Wim Loeb had taken from the cans were the duplicate shots which had either been taken twice or which were copies delivered to Westerbork from the Agfa developing laboratory in Arnhem. "I decided then," Loeb went on, "to edit a film that would show the story of Camp Westerbork from A to Z. I would smuggle the duplicated pieces of film out of the camp. But naturally I had to take care that one complete film remained in the camp, just in case camp commandant Gemmeker came and asked me for it."

Loeb had edited the film material fairly randomly; not in any logical order, but so "it would be a film worth seeing, telling a particular story."

On one occasion, however, he acted more purposefully. "I remember editing the girl between the wagon doors as end shot in the film. I cannot imagine there were any other shots of that girl, apart from those few seconds that really had no beginning and no end. I didn't throw anything of any worth away, especially not material as striking as that of the child who stood looking out of a wagon as the train drew out. Anyway, the image of the girl didn't particularly move me at that time, not as it does now. It struck me professionally as a good film shot, but I had experienced too much myself to be really touched by the girl's loneliness, uncertainty and possible fear."

Wim Loeb thought this section of the Westerbork film with the *perron scenes*, platform scenes, shown so often

51

after the war, had been put together from various film shots of different transports.

I told him that his supposition was right. The first one and a half minutes of the film section, *Eingang und Abfahrt,* comprises pictures of a passenger train coming from Amsterdam, from which new inmates for Westerbork disembark. The following two minutes show how shaven male prisoners from Vught concentration camp were brought to Westerbork by goods train and checked in by the *Registratur*. However, the remaining four minutes and forty-two seconds show inmates boarding a train consisting mainly of goods wagons with a few passenger coaches. The film ends with the long train leaving the camp with its engine, passenger coaches and wagons — destination Auschwitz and Bergen-Belsen.

Wim Loeb realised that the film he had edited would have to be signed over to the German authorities in Westerbork, probably to Gemmeker himself. Loeb couldn't remember whether that had happened or who had been involved. "I was told later, by whom I don't know, that the Germans took this film with them when they abandoned the camp in April 1945, and that those Germans, including Gemmeker, later fell into the hands of the Canadians. The Canadians would have taken the film from them."

The film — that is: the one that Wim Loeb had edited for camp commandant Gemmeker, the film that tells the story of the camp from "A to Z". But in his workhut, Loeb had put together a second, subversive film, from the duplicate fragments of film in his possession. "A film which didn't only show that cheerful work on the land, the farm and the sawing of Drente trees, but also, as I so clearly remember, definitely had shots of the transport. By combining the shots in this way I wanted to ensure that the confused events in Westerbork would be preserved for posterity."

Wim Loeb had given two or three cannisters containing the duplicated pieces of film to members of the Contact-Commissie. These were people who, during the last few months of the existence of the Westerbork Jewish Durchgangslager, had been allowed to go to Amsterdam a few times to visit their office.

As he spoke about the Contact-Commissie, Loeb mentioned the names of Hanauer, Eckmann, Heynemann and Grünberg. Or to be more accurate, his wife came out with their names and Wim Loeb agreed with her. Mrs Loeb had more memories than him of the members of that society, who, as I read later in Presser, had also been called the *Cognac-Commissie* because of their exuberant life style. Without faltering Wim Loeb said to me; "I have never trusted those people and I still don't."

He had succeeded in reporting to his wife that he had smuggled part of the film out of the camp via the Contact-Commissie, and had asked Mrs Loeb to go and check if the films had arrived in good order. This woman, who had not shrunk from going to The Hague and confronting a high SS officer like Willy Zöpf in his study, now turned up before the men of the Contact-Commissie. Mrs Loeb continued: "They had an office in Amsterdam-Zuid, and in the *hongerwinter* (Oct '44 — April '45, the period when the population of western Holland was starving) I saw them stuffing themselves like animals. There was nothing kosher about that."

It must have been in March 1945, she thought, that she went to the Contact-Commissie to ask what had happened to the film. She was told the material had been lost. The office had been raided by the police, and before the cops had stormed in, the films had been quickly tossed into a stove to prevent their discovery and removal

Wim Loeb looked at me and winked. "Of course that can't have happened," he said. "The film was celluloid and that stuff burnt and stank and smelt like hell! I'm sure they hung on to the film to use it once the war was over. To make themselves out to be heroes after all. 'Look at what we've preserved for history from Westerbork!' Really! Whatever happened, I have never seen that part of the Westerbork film again."

53

The afternoon drew to a close. Wim Loeb had an appointment and had to leave soon. Mrs Loeb had been out of the room a couple of times and was rattling pots and pans in the kitchen. My tape of the Westerbork film was still in its cassette box. It was now too late for us to watch the film together so I decided to to leave it with Wim Loeb for a while.

I was sure that he would watch the film more than once when he was alone, forwarding it and playing it back. Perhaps then a few doors would open in the depths of his memory.

Chapter 8

Was Sie mir da zeigen kenne ich noch nicht. I don't know anything about what you've just shown me

Thursday morning 9th December 1948. Outside, the wintry weather was bright and clear, but inside the huge court room of the regional Court of Law on the Brink in Assen it was dark. The curtains were drawn and the court room's upper windows were covered with improvised blackout paper. There was a film projector at the back of the hall, and a white screen had been placed near the raised platform where the judges of the Chamber of Drente of the Special Court of Leeuwarden were sitting. This Court had been established in May 1945 to handle all cases of war crimes and collaboration in the three northern provinces of Holland. All the seats in the courtroom were occupied.

The person about to be tried was the German Gemmeker, the former camp commander of Westerbork. Tall and slim, he was dressed in a grey uniform from which his military decorations and SS runes had been stripped. His grey hair, grown thinner during his three years in prison, had been combed back smoothly. He grasped a file of notes under his right arm. Standing before the court he confirmed politely, in a firm voice, that he was Albert Konrad Gemmeker, born on 27th September 1907 in Düsseldorf, Germany.

"Do you understand Dutch?" asked Judge A. Maarseveen, the chairman of the special punishment court.

"*Jawohl*," answered Gemmeker, "but I speak it badly."

The Procurator Fiscal, F. de Ranitz, began to read out the charges in Dutch; Gemmeker did not need a translation of the legal terms. The German, as commandant of Camp Westerbork, was accused of contravening the laws of war and humanity, and sending Jews off to foreign concentration camps, "simply and only because of the fact that they were of Jewish descent." This act led to the death of roughly one hundred thousand Jews.

Gemmeker had given the order to shoot dead a number of people who had tried to escape from Westerbork. Also, according to the Procurator Fiscal, he had ordered the carrying out of reprisals. Although his superiors in Amsterdam and The Hague had decided on a weekly quota of Jewish deportees, Gemmeker had once, as a punishment, forced an extra number of Jews onto the train. This, according to the charge, had led to the death of these deportees.

The Procurator Fiscal finished speaking. Now President Maarseveen spoke to Gemmeker. "Accused, during that time you authorized the making of a film about the activities in Westerbork, including the transports. To illustrate what we are dealing with, we will now show part of that film, the arrivals at the camp and the transports from it."

The lights in the hall went out, the film projector was set up and after some numbers and codes had come onto the screen, a locomotive was seen arriving at a camp on the Drente plain. Then people were seen; uniformed Germans, Dutch Military Police, and Jews, packed and ready to go, prisoners from Camp Westerbork. Some prisoners stood or sat in the wagons, others prepared to get into the train.

A number of people in the court room were overcome with emotion as the film progressed; some burst out sobbing, others left the hall. A journalist jotted down notes that he would later work into sentences: "Then we saw in this film the SS-thugs who accompanied the transports. Gemmeker in full glory, with his showy cap, ballooning jodhpurs and polished shining boots, his cronies buttoned up in the same fashion. It still makes our hair stand on end when we recall how these men ruled, the manner in which these men intended to execute their task. It was terrible during those years..."

The film presentation was at an end; the lamps were switched on again, but the court room remained dim. Gemmeker, who had been sitting on a chair so he could see the film properly, was led back to the dock.

The President said to him; "The fact, Prisoner, that you allowed the film to be made, proves that you were not touched by the deeply tragic fate of these people."

Gemmeker: *"Jawohl, gerade, Herr President!"*

President: "Just so?"

I translate the declaration that Gemmeker made in German:

"With this film, in which I let them include everything that happened in the camp, I wanted to make a film that was meant <u>for</u> the camp. For this reason I wanted to include everything, even the sorrow — so that it could never be said that I only allowed the better sides of the camp to be filmed — like the revues and the sport and so on — but also the sorrow."

President: "But what was your purpose in making this film?"

Gemmeker: "To record everything in the camp and to show it to the inmates. It was indeed shown to the inmates, although it was never fully completed."

President: "Wasn't it intended for your superiors?"

Gemmeker: "No. The inmate Todtmann wrote a script for it. He thought it should be shown to newcomers on entering the camp, to show all the things in the camp. Only the film did not get finished."

President: "The title of the film excerpt is a tragic statement, *Eingang und Abfahrt.*"

Gemmeker: "I have never seen it before, Mr President, there were a lot of excerpts (*Geschichte*) made that should have been shown to me for my approval — for inclusion in the film or not. I don't know anything about what you've just shown me."

Was Sie mir da zeigen kenne ich noch nicht. How enigmatic Gemmeker's words sounded on the morning of 9th

57

December 1948! He had just watched the images that so clearly and terribly illustrated the meaning implicit in the word "deportees" used in the the charges against him.

But Gemmeker claimed he did not recognise the pictures. I asked myself if he was speaking the truth. Or had he edited out these proposed pictures of the incoming and outgoing transports in the *Vorschläge für einen Film über Lager Westerbork,* before approving the synopsis in March or April 1944?

Or had the use of the "Pictures" proposed by Breslauer and/or Todtmann been permitted, along with the *Text*: "From July 1942, for almost two years, again and again the same picture: Transport"?

From Gemmeker's words from the dock it could even be deduced that he had ordered the pictures to be shot — as he wanted "to include everything, including the sorrow — so that it could never be said that I only allowed the better sides of the camp to be filmed..."

Nevertheless, he had just said: *"Was Sie mir da zeigen kenne ich noch nicht."*

I was getting nowhere during those days I spent sitting at my desk with cuttings from the *Asser Courant* of December 1948 and the stenographer's report of Gemmeker's trial. What were these other pictures that Gemmeker had not seen? The President had spoken about the film excerpt *Eingang und Abfahrt*. It has no context — it is quite different from the pieces of film showing the work in the barracks, where prisoners sit over batteries, chiseling or picking off silver layers of paper, the long scenes of shoe makers and brush makers, the laundry and smithy or the almost idyllic shots of life on the farm. The nine and a half minute excerpt *Eingang und Abfahrt* has not been edited. And it also contains the seven seconds of the girl in the door opening of the train wagon.

I was inclined to believe Gemmeker's words. Even though he <u>had</u> wanted to show "the sorrow of the camp as well", he would have considered the picture of the girl too extreme, because of the "terrible accusation" it contained, as Presser had later described it in *Ondergang*. Or was I overestimating Gemmeker's discernment? I felt convinced that Gemmeker — sentenced to ten years imprisonment in January 1949 but set free in 1955 — had seen those transport pictures, including his own masterful strutting on the Westerbork platform, for the first time that morning in the court room of Assen.

But which film had been shown?

Not the edited film that Wim Loeb had made in autumn 1944 in case Gemmeker should come by to ask him about it. According to Loeb, that had been a "watchable film that told a particular story." Had *Eingang und Abfahrt* perhaps been composed from the duplicated pieces of film that Wim Loeb had wanted to smuggle out of Westerbork to the Contact-Commissie? But those films had been dumped in an oven in Amsterdam-Zuid.

What sort of film documentary is it, the one that we now know as the "Westerbork film", those four scenes which altogether run for just under seventy minutes?

René Kok had still not been able to learn from the Rijksinstituut voor Oorlogsdocumentatie how the so called Westerbork film, now in the Institute's collection, had come to be found — who brought the film in, when and in what form.

I fretted about it, I could not make any progress. And moreover: after three months I still wasn't getting anywhere with the actual aim of my search — the name of the girl. It was becoming increasingly necessary for me to find out the date of the transport filmed by Breslauer. Spring 1944, March, April or May — that is all I knew. The girl had been taken from Westerbork in one of the five transports of that period.

In May 1993 I visited Wim Loeb for the second time. He still had the RVD videotape that I had left him more than two months before. Loeb received me very warmly but he was extremely busy that day and could not spare me much time. His wife had gone into town and he had arranged to meet her later in the centre of Haarlem. Yes, he had watched the film a few times, forwarding and reversing it and then reversing and forwarding it again: he had also slowed and paused some frames.

Loeb sat down on a chair by the open garden doors and looked at me pityingly. "I'm going to disappoint you again," he said, "as I did the first time you came to see me. Because I had nothing to do with the making of scenes Two, Three and Four of the film."

He gave me back the box with the videotape. "And as for the first part, in which the transports can be seen," he went on, "that is not the film I edited. It is clearly surplus material, so this could be the material I gave to the Contact-Commissie, so that they could send it to my wife to keep for me until after the liberation."

Wim Loeb apologised that he could not be more precise. His memory occasionally let him down, he said, he had possibly suppressed all kind of things. And that suppression, he added, had been really successful, because, and here he tapped the wooden arm of his chair, he was now seventy-seven, and forty-eight years had passed since the liberation of Westerbork, and yet he had never suffered from that notorious KZ syndrome *(Konzentrationslager Syndrome)* about which he had heard so much.

Then he pointed to the videocassette in my hand and said: "The film I made was a much longer film than the one you have there. It also contains pictures of the transports, but the images are better. And as for that girl in the train wagon you're always talking about, I used that footage in the film as end-shot. I don't feel the loss of those pictures as much as I regret the loss of the other tranport pictures. But I told you that last time."

"What's happened to your film?" I asked Loeb, trying to hide the despair in my voice; "the film which told 'the story of the camp from A to Z', with the girl in the train wagon as end-shot?"

"As far as I know," said Wim Loeb, "the film was handed over to the Canadians at the Liberation. But it could be that it's just something I heard and have made into a real memory. Don't judge me too harshly for that. There is one more thing I would really like to say to you: I've watched the videotape three or four times, looked at it carefully. I find it awful, I also find it collaborative. I could never have made such a film."

In the car on the way home, I felt at odds with myself. Was there nothing else on which I could expend my energy? I was still almost daily on the go for my newspaper — couldn't I use my clearly overzealous journalistic capacity in a better way and get involved with a more rewarding project?

Was there no other subject to deal with apart from the image of the girl, couldn't I find another stimulating subject to plumb to the very depths?

In the evening I sat despondently at home, reading through all the notes I had made over the last three months. Then I remembered a remark René Kok had made when we were in the filmbunker in Scheveningen; in April or May 1944 there was also a "Gypsy transport" which left Westerbork in a combined train taking people to Auschwitz, Bergen-Belsen, Theresienstadt and Ravensbrück.

Although I still didn't know how to continue my search, I decided to try to find out what part the "Gypsy transport" had played in the history of Camp Westerbork.

Chapter 9

The *Auschwitz-Erlass* (Auschwitz Decree)

The people known as *Zigeuners* (Gypsies), live dispersed throughout the entire world. There are now an estimated five million Gypsies; people with a more or less common language and culture. Roughly a third live in Europe, mainly in the eastern parts of that continent. The Gypsies are romantically known as wandering folk, but since the twentieth century, a number have chosen to live in huge camping areas with modern facilities, often alongside "white" caravaners.

When the Germans began their occupation of Holland on 15th May 1940, the National Register of Population mentioned that there were between 2,700 and 3,000 caravans in the country, and 11,000 to 12,000 caravan dwellers. The Gypsies and other caravan dwellers were found mainly in the southern provinces of Noord-Brabant and Limburg.

The German National Socialist Party had implemented an anti-Gypsy policy in their homeland, based on the Nuremberg racial laws of 1935. So Gypsies, like Jews, lost their civil rights, and on 8th September 1938, Himmler, the SS leader, declared that Gypsies were a special problem group, like Jews, and a final solution, *eine Endlösung*, should be applied to them.

With the invasion of Poland which led to the start of the Second World War, the Germans started to expel 2,800 German Gypsies to ghettos in conquered Poland. A year later Gypsies were forbidden to marry Aryans, and the subject of the mass sterilisation of Gypsies was brought up.

In January 1943, after a year in which Gypsies and half-Gypsies (*Mischlinge*) suffered more injustices, Reichsführer-SS Heinrich Himmler issued his *Auschwitz-Erlass*. This ordered the deportation of German and non-German Gypsies to Poland. In February 1943, the first group was sent to the Gypsy Camp of the Auschwitz II complex in Birkenau; by July 1944, 21,000 Gypsies from Germany and Austria had been sent there.

In Holland many public servants — including some who were not members of the Dutch Nazi Party (NSB) — saw their chance to implement an anti-Gypsy policy, and shortly after the German occupation, asked the German authorities for permission to put caravan dwellers into special camps. They got their way in 1943 when a Restriction of Movement Order was imposed and twenty-seven collection camps were set up. Less than half the caravan dwellers, however, went to live in the camps.

Most of the Gypsies sold or hid their wagons and settled in abandoned houses — the majority of which had been officially declared unfit for habitation — in The Hague on the Veenkade and in the Bilderdijkstraat. Some found accommodation in Amsterdam in the now largely evacuated Jewish area in the centre of the city. Other Gypsies tried to remain outside the collection camps by appealing to the regional police commanders for exemption from the Restriction of Movement Order, so they could continue to practice their roaming lifestyle as entertainers. A number of Gypsies went underground.

Himmler's *Auschwitz-Erlass* of early 1943 stated that the deportation to concentration camps also applied to Gypsies in Holland, Belgium, Alsace-Lorraine and Luxemburg. The German occupiers of Holland however, had not been in a hurry to carry out Himmler's command. In 1943 the German and Dutch police authorities had their hands full with many other matters. Furthermore, the majority of Dutch caravan dwellers were not classed as Gypsies.

The *Auschwitz-Erlass* found its way into the desk drawers of various police offices, resurfacing only on 14th May

1944 to result in an urgent and secret telex report to the five regional Police Chiefs of Holland.

This report read: "In order to carry out the centralised arrest of all those remaining in Holland who can be identified as Gypsies, all Gypsy families, including children, must, by order of the Befehlshaber der Ordnungspolizei, be picked up by the Dutch Police on Tuesday 16 May 1944 from 07.00 hours onwards and dispatched to Camp Westerbork by 20.00 hours at the latest. The above applies to all people, who on grounds of their appearance, customs and habits can be identified as Gypsies or half-Gypsies, including all those who travel around in the Gypsy fashion."

The order was transmitted immediately to the police, the Dutch Military Police and the *Landwacht* (a paramilitary force of Dutch Nazi volunteers), and was executed by them without further delay. Collection camps in fifteen areas of Holland were surrounded in the early morning of 16 May 1944, as were houses and individual caravans where Gypsies might be living.

On that day 578 Gypsies were arrested: men, women and many children. In the course of 16th and 17th May the prisoners were taken to Assen by various trains. In Assen they had to board a train to Westerbork.

In the camp, 279 of the group were found not to be Gypsies, but merely caravan dwellers. They were freed on 20th May. Of the rest of the group of 299 Gypsies, it appeared that 54 carried passports from neutral or Allied countries. They were also able to leave on 20th May.

One day earlier, however, in the morning of 19th May 1944, the 245 who were not caravan dwellers and who did not hold passports from non-Dutch states, were forced into cattle and goods wagons. These took the Gypsies and 208 Jews from Westerbork to Auschwitz. The same locomotive drew the passenger compartment transporting 238 Jews, headed for the Bergen-Belsen concentration camp.

Chapter 10

Dismay, quest abandoned

"If in the spring of 1944 Breslauer did indeed film a transport leaving for Auschwitz and Celle, as stated on that piece of paper from your Rijksinstituut voor Oorlogsdocumentatie, then it <u>must have been</u> the train of 19th May 1944!

"Take a good look at the list of the transports made in March, April and May 1944; on 15th March a train with 210 people went to Bergen-Belsen... On 23rd March the train had only one destination — Auschwitz. That day 509 people were sent there from Westerbork. On 5th April a train travelled with people for three different camps; 289 went to Theresienstadt, 240 to Auschwitz and 101 to Bergen-Belsen.

"And then there's that train of 19th May 1944, taking 238 people to Bergen-Belsen and 453 to Auschwitz. On 3rd June yet another train left Westerbork with 496 people for Auschwitz. From then until 31 July, at the height of summer — a fact which would have been clearly evident on the film — no other train left Westerbork.

"In the filmed train there are two distinct groups of passengers; one group occupying the passenger compartments and a large group getting into goods and cattle wagons, or already sitting in them. The people in the passenger compartments are going to Bergen-Belsen; they look more or less like normal train passengers. This illusion of normality, also created at the deportation to Theresiendstadt, the camp in Czechoslovakia, comes from using passenger compartments.

"Therefore I have no doubt that the film shots are of the transport of 19th May 1944, which implies that the girl in the door opening of the wagon is not a Jewish child, but a Gypsy girl. This answers the question as to why no one from the surviving community recognised her after the war. And I have a few reasons for this theory!"

Listen to Wagenaar having a violent argument with René Kok! I was once again visiting the administrator of the film archives of the Oorlogsdocumentatie. I was walking angrily up and down the huge 17th century drawing room on the Herengracht, where every day Kok sat in front of two desks covered with all kinds of documents, studying images of the past. I was using Kok as a sounding board.

I had hacked through some of my doubts a few days earlier. I now believed that the filmed transport in the Westerbork film was of the train of 19 May 1944. I was also almost sure that the isolated seven seconds of the film with the girl between the wagon doors had been shot by Breslauer, or an assistant, near that part of the train in which 245 Gypsies had waited before their departure from Westerbork.

This had to be the only piece of film of the Gypsy transport. The shot of the child in the door opening is so completely different in atmosphere and character from the footage of the bustling platform, with all the people getting ready, either with or without assistance, to leave Westerbork, or who were already on board the wagons.

"You know," I said to René Kok, " there are many other people shown in the wagons of the Westerbork film. Sometimes they're talking to someone on the platform, and that too is quite dramatic. But what makes that one shot so powerful is the girl's dreadful loneliness, the terror in her eyes, her small head beneath the cloth, her awful vulnerability. The child doesn't seem to be a part of her surroundings. Of course, all the people outside the train make up a pitiful group, but you don't see anyone else who is completely alone. But the girl; she's lonely and anonymous. And there weren't any anonymous Jews, young or old, in Westerbork in the spring of 1944."

[handwritten margin note:] vulnerable (significant point)

[handwritten note at bottom:] gypsies as an afterthought

I read out information I had copied from the book by Lou de Jong, the former director of the Rijksinsituut, and from Presser's *Ondergang,* to René Kok.

In the first period of the establishment of Westerbork as a Polizeiliches Juden Durchgangslager from July 1942 to the end of February 1943, fifty-one trains left the camp. They all went to Auschwitz transporting over 44,000 Jews. From 2nd March to 20 July 1943, nineteen trains went to Sobibor, carrying over 34,000 Jews. Following that period, up to 23 March 1944, another 14,000 Jews were taken from Westerbork to Auschwitz, Bergen-Belsen and Theresienstadt.

"The tempo was especially fast in Westerbork in 1942 and 1943," I said to René Kok. He was aware of that, of course, and listened with a grunt, a little taken aback — because I was sounding a bit like an annoying windbag, I could hear it myself.

In the beginning, the aim of the Germans in Berlin, The Hague and Amsterdam — Himmler, Eichmann, Zöpf, Aus der Fünten and those other evil scum— was to transport the greatest possible number of Jews as quickly as possible from Holland to the places of the *Endlösung*.

"That was the period of the deportation of the Jewish masses, particularly the tens of thousand mainly anonymous members of Dutch Jewry. Those people who, as Mr Cohen had told us, came from "the Jewish proletariat which before the war, made up the greatest part of Amsterdam Jewry."

They were the poor souls, unknown and nameless beyond their wretched basements in Amsterdam's Jewish area. They were not members of Jewish society, they were not wealthy or well-placed — they were not retired and financially independent, not investors, doctors or celebrated medical specialists, famous Bühne artistes, painters or violinists in the famous Concertgebouworkest, they were not traders; they didn't even have a market stall on the Waterlooplein.

The face of the girl with the headcloth could have merged with the faces of countless other anonymous children from the Jewish proletariat in the great mass of Jews leaving Westerbork in 1942 and 1943. But not in the spring of 1944!"

I continued with my objections.

I said that according to the historians, all the Jews without property or other means of support had left Westerbork by the beginning of the third year of the deportations. The hour of departure had now come for those Jews who up to then had been exempt from getting on the train because of their special status. These people were known as — awful word — the "privileged"; people who had managed to get a place on one of many "lists" because their presence in Holland had been useful for the Germans. For example; on account of previous service to the German State or because they had a special link through a relative to one or other emigration land — or because they had paid a lot of money for a place on one of the lists.

For that reason, they had been *zurückgestellt* in Westerbork — temporarily exempted from the transports. And when at last the train *did* come for them, it took them mainly to Bergen-Belsen or Theresienstadt, camps which didn't have such a bad name as Auschwitz or Sobibor. Westerbork inmates knew that Bergen-Belsen served as an *Austauschlager* (exchange camp) for Jews who might, for example, go on to the British Mandate of Palestine. And Theresienstadt particularly had always been known to be a *Vorzügslager*, a model camp about which a film had been made by the Jewish director Kurt Gerron, who by the way, was also imprisoned in Westerbork for a while. His film is called *Der Führer schenkt den Juden eine Stadt* (The Führer gives the Jews a Country).

I read aloud to René Kok from the second half of part 8 of the masterly work of his former boss Lou de Jong, the founder and long serving manager of the Rijksinstituut voor Oorlogsdocumentatie.

"This is to illustrate what kind of people were taken from Westerbork in 1944, after the masses had left in 1942 and 1943. It says here," and I quoted loosely, "that in the classified groups making up the Theresienstadt transport of 18th January 1944, there were 13 German ex-soldiers from the First World War with 105 of their relatives. Plus 53 Jews, including relatives, who had served the Reich in other ways.

"Also taken to Theresienstadt were 70 half-Jews and 58 children whose parents were already there. Then there is mention of another *"55 Jüdische Elternteile aus nicht mehr bestehenden Mischehen mit halbarischen Kindern"* — I can't make out this German underworld jargon, but I don't think that one can speak of anonymity here.

"There were two other specific groups on this train of 18th January 1944. These were the 141 parents of people who had given exceptional service during the *Entjudung* of Holland and the Westerbork camp, and the 351 people who had distinguished themselves in the administration and management of Camp Westerbork. The number 351 includes relatives.

"Can you imagine such a pitiful, lonely and vulnerable girl at the wagon door belonging to such a special group of Westerborkers?" I asked Kok. "Or could she have been one of the 3,650 Jews sent from Westerbork to Bergen-Belsen? I read that 100 to 200 Jews had passports from South American countries, 1,200 Jews had bought the so-called 120,000 stamp for twenty to thirty thousand guilders in gold, jewellery or diamonds, thus exempting themselves from the transports for such a long time. The group also contained 800 Jews with dual Dutch-British nationality, 450 Jews who were eligible for exchange with the author-ities of the British Mandate in Palestine, and 350 Jews who the Germans hoped would set up a diamond cutting shop in Bergen-Belsen."

René Kok finally said something in reply: "Anne Frank and her family were among the 1,019 passengers on the transport of September 3rd 1944, the last that went to

Auschwitz from Westerbork. You can't say that the Frank family hadn't done their best to live in complete anonymity."

The objection was one that I had already put to myself.

"I think that these families were the only ones you could call nameless amongst the Jews sent on the twenty-one trains leaving Westerbork in 1944. These were Jews who had gone underground and who, through betrayal or carelessness, had been hauled from their hiding places in the last stages of the German *Entjudung* of Holland.

"These fugitives were arrested as S-cases (*Straf Fälle*) — prisoners awaiting punishment — taken to Westerbork, and locked in a special barrack while waiting for the first train able to accommodate them. And often their heads were shaved, men, women and children. Naturally I wondered about the headcloth of the girl in the door opening of the wagon; did the cloth hide a bald head — was the girl a punished fugitive, a girl like Anne Frank?

"But how could it be that after the war, when the film of the girl going to Auschwitz in the wagon was shown on television for the umpteenth time, no one had ever come forward to say they recognised her? Someone, for example, who had hidden the child or members of her family in his house. Or someone from the small group of Jews who had returned to Holland after the liberation — or a loved one who was drawn by some kinship to that little face?

"The girl between the wagon doors with her terrified frightened face is perhaps as familiar to millions of people as Anne Frank with her diary. A few years ago a documentary film maker managed to find seven Jewish women who had met Anne Frank in Westerbork, Auschwitz or Bergen-Belsen. But the sight of the film or a photo of the girl in the wagon door has never brought anyone forward to declare, 'I know that child on the train! Or: I believe I know her.' For almost fifty years she's remained just a frightened, terrified, nameless girl with a headcloth on.

"So, now I know she's not a Jewish child but one of the girls from the Gypsy transport of 19 May 1944. Sure, none of the community of survivors or their relatives has ever come forward and claimed to recognise her, but I don't find that so strange. Because the members of the small Gypsy community which remains in Holland have withdrawn into their shell. Apart from a time some years ago, when Professor Sijes and a group of his students approached them, they've never been asked about their memories of the years of persecution and the annihilation of their families."

"It's possible you're on to something," said René Kok after a long silence. "But," he went on, denting my confidence a little, "it's unbelievable how many people on photos taken during the war aren't recognised for a really long time, then one day, out of the blue, someone reports that they know them."

Kok took a pile of photos from the great table in the middle of his office and randomly spread them out. There were about forty, forming a photo reportage of the raid of 26th May 1943. That was the day when three thousand Jews from the centre of Amsterdam were rounded up and herded to Muiderpoortstation and the Olympiaplein. There they had to wait some hours until trams and trains could be organised to take them to Westerbork.

René Kok showed me the photo of a solitary young woman. She is standing holding a bottle of water, a jacket over her right arm, a Jewish Star on the upper left of her short-sleeved dress. She looks round searchingly, her glasses perched on her long nose.

"This photo is quite well known and has been published internationally because it tells a story," said Kok. "It also appears in the *Encylopedia Judaica*, with the inscription, 'Woman with Dutch Jewish Star'. But it wasn't until June 1987 that I received a letter from someone claiming to know her. A man from Hoogeveen wrote that her name was Eva Granada, and she'd worked as a nurse in the Nieuw Israëlitisch Ziekenhuis, the hospital in Amsterdam, and been deported to Auschwitz in 1943.

"What I mean is this: forty-four years after the raid of May 1943 someone said, 'Heh, I know her!' Why didn't he let himself know her earlier? Perhaps the human memory has its reasons: everything in its time. So I find your theory about 'never recognised and therefore not a Jewish girl,' plausible but not completely convincing."

By this time I knew that in order to find out who that girl in the door opening is or was, I had to seek out her relatives or maybe survivors from the group of Dutch Gypsies who had returned from Westerbork.

Rudolf Breslauer had shot his film of the train on May 19 1944. Mrs Lenie Cohen-Nijstad, who appears in the film as a young woman serving in the Fliegende Kolonne, must have been mistaken when she told me that she had not worked on 19th May 1944. She had told me a couple of weeks ago that in April 1944 she had had a bout of jaundice, but had been able to resume work in the second half of May. She had obviously been in Westerbork on 19th May 1944, she must have forgotten — or maybe there was a mistake in the Westerbork work sheets she was using to jog her memory.

In the evening I phoned the Cohen family in Amsterdam. When Jules Cohen came on the line I told him that I was absolutely convinced that the transport from Westerbork in the Breslauer film had taken place on 19th May 1944. A group of 245 Gypsies had been sent to Auschwitz on that day.

"If your wife has another think and you go through your album carefully together, you should find that she was indeed present on that day, 19th May. Otherwise she couldn't have been in the film. Moreover it was your wife who first mentioned the Gypsy transport from Westerbork. She told René Kok about it on the phone after our visit."

Jules Cohen said, "Yes, that could well be. I'll put your question to my wife."

Two hours later Cohen rang back.

"Mr Wagenaar, I'm sorry about your investigation, but my wife was <u>not</u> at the train on 19th May 1944. Although she was still recovering from jaundice, she *was* working that day, but outside the camp — my wife spent the whole day working as a cleaner in Port Natal in Assen, she is absolutely clear about this. That was an institution for mental patients which the Germans were using for their own purposes.

"There is no possible doubt," Cohen told me. "My wife was filmed serving as a member of the Fliegende Kolonne at the train on another day, not 19th May 1944. Which other day that was, neither of us know."

The film excerpt had therefore not been shot on May 19th 1944 — so the girl between the doors of the wagon was not one of the Gypsies transported to Auschwitz from Westerbork on that day. It was 21st April 1993. I felt defeated and decided to abandon my search for the name of the girl once and for all.

Chapter 11

Advent in Berlin

It was December 1993, the year was almost over. More than seven months had passed since April, during which time I had thought about the lonely girl in the Westerbork film almost every day. At the beginning of my search I'd been given a photo of the girl by the Westerbork Herrineringscentrum (Remembrance Centre). I often took the photo from my wallet and looked at the child's face for a while. Then I put it away; mission not accomplished, pity, regret and also some guilt.

Shortly after I had given up my search, I was sent part one of the so called *Westerbork Cahiers*, a book which now appears annually with essays about the history of the former Jewish Durchgangslager in Drente. On page 53 the girl from the train looked out at me once more from her wagon, her photo illustrating an article by Ben Prinsen about Hertha Aussen, another girl from Camp Westerbork, whose short, barely seventeen-year life the Remembrance Centre researchers had been able to reconstruct.

Almost irritated, I read the introductory lines which had been placed next to the photo of the child between the wagon doors.

Here we went again: "The face of a girl. Apparently calm. So might any child look. Open to the future. But yet, there is more than that. There's an expression of incomprehension. Of a certain resigned helplessness. Of fear, also. Yes, of a sorrow over the loss of everything that is dear. And of the uncertainty about what is to come..."

And then, inevitably; "The photo raises many questions. Who is this girl? What is is she thinking and feeling? Why the helplessness? What has become of her?"

I was struck by my annoyance on reading the article; was I right to have given up? Should I really have yielded so easily just because of the Cohens' announcement that the date of the film could not have been 19th May 1944? Surely that didn't negate the fact that either Breslauer or someone else had aimed a camera on a certain day at the girl in the wagon, a child who had an official name and a pet name? Keep on looking then!

But I did not. I no longer called up on my computer screen the directory "Esther" with its eighteen files, containing the many, many notes resulting from my long months of research.

At the beginning of November I received a letter from a Koert Broersma from Assen. I knew Broersma's name as his biography of Philip Mechanicus had recently been published. I hadn't read the book yet, but my chief editor had written a very laudatory review about *Buigen onder de storm* (Bow beneath the storm). Philip Mechanicus was a Jewish journalist on the Amsterdam daily newspaper *Algemeen Handelsblad*, who from 28th May 1943 to the middle of 28th February 1944, had recorded a diary of daily life in the camp in thirteen exercise books, adding his own comments. After the war, Mechanicus's diary was published in Dutch under the title *In Depôt*, and also widely read in translation abroad.

With this biography, according to my chief editor, Koert Broersma had succeeded in producing a major literary work about Mechanicus, which complemented the masterpiece that the diary itself already formed — it was almost unbelievable that the author, as a historian as well as a writer, should be a so-called amateur.

Broersma informed me in his letter that he had recently started researching the background of a film made by Breslauer in 1944. He understood that I had been investigating a specific excerpt from this film: "the girl between the wagon doors". So he would much appreciate it if we could meet and exchange ideas. Broersma had seen the complete film shots several times and had also drawn a few tentative conclusions of his own regarding the shot of "the girl".

He hoped to make an appointment with me as soon as possible. *Ach*, I thought to myself, why not? I did feel however, that someone was about to run off with my girl. On the other hand; the man in Assen was evidently only interested in the film and however deeply he immersed himself in the subject, he would be unable to get any closer to the girl on the train than me. I rang Broersma and invited him round.

The conversation that we had a few days later lasted for almost four hours, and I was exhausted when Broersma got up to leave. I did almost all the talking, it was as if I was lying on a psychiatrist's couch. I related my search to him with an enthusiasm that I had to temper every few minutes; I told him of the dozens of times I'd played the video of the film, the hours I'd spent shut up with the correspondence of Breslauer and others, my meeting with the Cohens, the search for Wim Loeb, the fascinating afternoon in the Scheveningen film bunker, the books I'd delved into, the discoveries I'd made — and how everything always raised more questions than answers.

Broersma said that he was very impressed. From his body language, I guessed he thought he was dealing with a complete monomaniac. He had been writing busily while I spoke. Now he said: "How sad it is that you've stopped. In my opinion, if you'd continued, you'd have found out the identity of the girl. Although I should add that no one from the Herrineringscentrum Kamp Westerbork reckons you have much of a chance."

Broersma then asked, a little shyly, what he might use from the information I'd given him for the purposes of his own search. "All of it," I said, adding that should he find out the exact date of the filmed transport while researching the history of the film, he would share this knowledge with me.

Koert Broersma promised solemnly to keep to the bargain and left for Assen. Our meeting took place on 17th November. I heard nothing more from him in the following weeks, nor did I expect to.

* * *

One month later, the week before Christmas, my family and I went to Berlin, a city I had visited about fifteen times since 1970. Before our departure, I discussed the itinerary with my wife and our two sons aged fifteen and eighteen, to ensure that we would spend some pleasantly varied days together enjoying the German capital; this meant plenty of time for shopping, visiting the Christmas markets near the Gedächtniskirche and the Alexanderplatz, and also ample opportunity for us to familiarise ourselves with Berlin and German history by some selective sightseeing — rather than coming across the past randomly, as I myself prefer, on every street corner.

In spite of this agreement however, I found myself getting out of my car alone one afternoon to visit the infamous villa which still stands on the little square near 56-58 Am Grossen Wannsee. My family had remained at the Kurfürstendamm. They thought that they had devoted quite enough time to historical pursuits the previous day, visiting the Topografie des Terrors, the ruins of the Gestapo headquarters and prisons, and the Headquarters of the Reich Security Bureau, (SS and Reichssicherheitshauptamt) on Prinz Albrechtstrasse, now called Niederkirchenstrasse.

The first thing that struck me as I entered the Wannsee villa was that all the villains, whose portraits were hanging on the wall of the dining room, had been so very young. They were mainly thirty-year olds, with a couple of forty-year olds, yuppies in a Europe that up to then had been ruled by old men with moustaches and goatees, top hats and canes. Not more than a couple of these fifteen Nazi criminals that I saw on the wall could

77

have been over fifty on 20 January 1944, the day of their fateful conference.

Their host, Reinhard Heydrich, chief of the Security Police of the SD, was thirty-eight; Dr Rudolf Lange, the SS Sturmbannführer who had been brought in from Latvia where he had murdered 60,000 Jews, was only thirty-two; Heinrich Müller, SS Gruppenführer and chief of Gestapo, was forty-two; Dr Eberhard Schöngarth, commander of the Security Police in Poland, was thirty-nine — and the man in the photo next to him, so well turned out in his smart uniform, was just thirty-seven. That was Adolf Eichmann, SS Obersturmbannführer and active in the Reichsicherheitshauptamt (Reich Security Head Office). Eichmann was to take the minutes of what was said in the villa that afternoon.

They were almost all men of the twentieth century, these board members of the society of murderers; young, diligent, and full of unbridled ambition. Could it have happened that these fifteen men, these SS Officers and top civil servants from Berlin, had taken only one and a half hours to reach an agreement about the carrying out of the death sentence of eleven million European Jews?

Yes, it had happened. Their decision is recorded in the pages of the report of the meeting of 20th January 1942, which took place at 12.00 in the villa on the Wannsee square. The typed *Besprechungsprotokoll* (Minutes) now lie under glass on a long table. It is a report which, with many-syllabled and sinister German words, ends with a draft of the *"organisatorischen, sachlichen und materiellen Belange im Hinblick auf die Endlösung der europäischen Judenfrage"* (organisational, essential and material consequences in consideration of the Final Solution of the matter of European Jews). That was the reason these fifteen men had gathered here: to discuss this matter and to set down on paper the plan for the definitive solution of the Jewish question.

In the invitation to the meeting he was to chair, Heydrich had promised that the proceedings would take place *"mit anschliessendem Frühstück"* — with the provision of an ample breakfast. For how much time could it take to draw up the outline? Not one of the fifteen men sitting round the table would want to further question the validity of liquidating eleven million people, no matter how it was to be carried out. That time-consuming moralising was over — there was now no doubt that only the physical destruction of the Jews would solve the problem they posed. All that remained to be done was to ensure that the murders would be carried out as as efficiently as possible, causing minimal damage to the German soul.

A couple of hours after Heydrich had opened the conference, the participants left the large villa with its coarse stucco plaster and the lifelike angels bordering the roof, and walked down the avenue with their stomachs full of brunch and their heads full of a sense of being chosen. They made their way along the gravel path to the large cars which stood waiting for them in the curve of the tree-lined road overlooking the lake.

Hurry, return to the centre of Berlin, leave the Wannsee, don't waste a minute! These officers and functionaries had much more to do on that January day in the war year 1942. And particularly for the diligent Adolf Eichmann, the hours of working were not yet over, and would continue well into the darkness of the night.

The high windows of the terrace of the Wannsee dining room overlooked the lake. Rowing boats covered half the surface of the water, and on the bank in the distance I could make out a grandstand beside a rowing course. Inside the villa I looked to my left, my glance resting on a poster from the Municipality of The Hague, the Dutch seat of government and royal residence.

"Notice is served of Duty of Application for people of Jewish blood," commands the Mayor, observing Item 1, Section Three and Art. 2, Section One of one or other evil decree. On work days from quarter to four to half four, Jews from The Hague had to get their application form at

60 Jan Hendrikstraat, 8a Stationsweg, 303 Beeklaan, 66 Anna Palownastraat, 342 Rijswijkseweg, 163-165 Apeldoornselaan, 32 Azaleastraat, and 255b Marcellisstraat.

The Duty of Application was introduced on 1st February 1941.

One year later, here, in the Wannsee villa, fifteen men, most of whom were young, drew up the routes and travel schemes leading from 32 Azaleastraat to Auschwitz, Sobibor or other extermination camps far from The Hague.

In other rooms of the Wannsee villa there were photos of the camps and transports, and pictures of the mass execution of Jews by SS Einsatztruppen (Special troops) — a bloody and continuous enterprise, that soon disgusted even the greatest monsters among them — so it was decided to use gas. I saw blueprints of drawings from German engineering offices for efficient, specifically designed camps with crematoria and gas chambers, along with calculations of capacity, estimates for the necessary infrastructure of these sites of mechanised mass murder, analysis of cost and benefit. How ingenious it all was!

The villa was in the southwest of Berlin, at the edge of the Grünewald, where the wide river Havel rests for a while in the Grosser Wannsee before continuing to flow northwards. The businessman Ernst Marlier was one of many rich Berliners to build a country house at the beginning of the twentieth century in this forested area full of lakes and rivers. His house, dating from 1914, measured fifteen hundred square metres and had a garden of forty thousand square metres. In November 1940, when Hitler had been in power in Germany for almost eight years — the charming villa was purchased for 1.9 million Reichsmark by the SS foundation Nordhav, as a holiday home for officers of the Security Service. The chief of the SD, Reinhard Heydrich, later acquired the villa as his private country house. That is why he acted as host and chairman at the conference of 20 January 1942, at which it was decided to murder the whole of European Jewry.

Six months after the Wannsee Conference the murder machine was in full swing in Eastern Europe, with trains from occupied Western Europe travelling punctually to the extermination camps. There, Jews were killed in the gas chambers, often just hours after arrival at their destination. In Auschwitz, the organisation had been so well perfected that ten thousand people could be gassed and their bodies burnt within twenty-four hours.

These facts were reiterated as I wandered round the villa 56-58 Am Grossen Wannsee. I also read the enthusiastic verdict on the finished job, written by the supervisor of the murderers, Reichsführer SS Himmler; *Es ist herrlich in einer Zeit zu leben die Ihren Menschen grosse Aufgaben stellt.* (It is splendid to live in a time which sets one's people such great challenges.)

After the German downfall in 1945, the Wannsee villa was briefly used as a shelter for Russian marines. In 1947, the American occupiers turned it into an Officers' Home. Later it served as a High School, and then the villa became a holiday centre for children from the Berlin area of Neukölln.

Not until the eighties was there a growing consciousness that the villa at 56-58 Am Grossen Wannsee was different from the hundreds of other splendid Berlin country houses around the lake. Although it took such a long time for its historical importance to be realised, the idea to purchase and restore the villa was undertaken with great zeal and it was turned into a place of memorial.

On 20th January 1992, fifty years after the conference of Heydrich and his cronies, the villa was thrown open to the public. Since then, as many as three thousand visitors a week, including many pupils and their teachers, have come to see if this conference really took place. After spending an hour and a half shuffling through the rooms the majority return to urban Berlin, bursting with more questions than they had when they arrived. This is what happened to me too. It was only on the Kurfürstendamm, as I turned right into Meinekestrasse where my guesthouse was situated, that it occurred to me that this was the first time I had not seen the photo of the girl at the wagon doors in an exhibition about the Holocaust. And I had not thought about her for the whole afternoon. I was shocked by this. What had happened to me — had I been released from my obsession?

Chapter 12

Kroon, Frouwke
26-9-1882 Appingedam
22-5-1944 Auschwitz

A few days after Christmas, the telephone rang. It was Koert Broersma sounding agitated, but happy to finally catch me at home. He reminded me of the solemn promise he had made when he visited me in November.

"I want to tell you," he said, "that we, Gerard Rossink from the Memorial Centre of Camp Westerbork and me, have positively confirmed that it was definitely on 19th May 1944 that Breslauer took his shots of the train. There's no possible doubt about the date; you were right; 19th May 1944! Come to Westerbork as soon as you can."

Two weeks passed before we managed to meet, and on 10th January 1994, I sceptically entered the main building of the Herinneringscentrum. A secretary led me directly to the library, where Broersma and Rossink were waiting for me with coffee and local Drente currant buns. But we didn't have time for eating and drinking. Rossink was eager to start up *Eingang und Abfahrt*, Scene 1 of the Westerbork film. On a screen on the wall were the pictures that I now knew so well; the locomotive steaming in, the people from Amsterdam disembarking, the shaven prisoners from Vught, a glimpse of the Registration Area, and the bustle on the platform next to the train going to Auschwitz and Bergen-Belsen.

The helper pushes the old woman on the stretcher with its bicycle wheels; once more he doesn't know which wagon he ought to go to and turns the homemade ambulance back again.

The film was stopped.

"Now in slow motion," said Koert Broersma, sounding triumphant. "Look, see here; there's a suitcase on the stretcher, look!"

Yes, I see it; there's a case lying on its side.

Broersma: "And there's something white on the case!"

Something white, yes; the case has an inscription.

"Can you read what it says?"

I can't.

"We couldn't either, at first," said Broersma, "but we paused the film, printed out the shot and had it enlarged. Then we were able to make out that P or F Kroon had been written on the case in chalk or white paint, with a birth date underneath: 26-9 and then 32, 82 or 92. This means the birth date was 26 September 1932 — but that would be impossible because then the invalid would only have been twelve — or 26th September 1882 or 26 September 1892 — that could well be; that would have made the sick woman sixty-two or fifty-two years old."

Then Koert Broersma laid a photocopy from the register of the War Graves' Foundation in front of me. The page was full of names, he had put a thick line under one of them: *Kroon, Frouwke 26-9-1882 Appingedam 22-5-1944 Auschwitz.*

"We applied to the Rijksinstituut voor Oorlogsdocumentatie for the transport lists from the Westerbork archives," said Broersma. He sounded moved and added solemnly, "From the lists it appeared that Mrs Frouwke Kroon, who lived at 64 Waalstraat in Amsterdam for most of the war, was sent from Westerbork to Auschwitz in the train of 19 May 1944. She died in Auschwitz on the 22nd May, 1944, just after her arrival."

This was a terrible fact Nevertheless, I congratulated Broersma and Rossink on their discovery. Then Rossink added: "By blowing up the film shots we found out another couple of things. Above the inscription *"74 Pers"* on the wagon where the girl is standing, the number 16 can be seen. The wagon is one of the five or six uncoupled units standing at the rear, while further up the platform the hustle continues as people board the train and the Germans constantly inspect everything. As the train moves off you see wagon 16 — where the girl is — clearly passing by. But now the passenger number has altered from 74 to 75. So the number of occupants must have been changed before the doors were closed. The figure was erased and the correct number was written on the side."

Koert Broersma said, "We've reached the same conclusion as you: they used the train section made up of wagons 11 or 12 to 16 or 17 to take 254 Dutch Gypsies to Auschwitz on 19 May."

In the evening, after returning home from Westerbork, I phoned Mrs Cohen to inform her about the definite confirmation of the date of the filmed transport. It was 19th May 1944, no possible doubt. I told her about Mrs Kroon's suitcase and she appeared to be moved.

We discussed exactly where Mrs Cohen is to be seen in the film. And at last the misunderstanding that had hindered me for so long and which had almost brought me to the point of giving up my search became obvious. It suddenly dawned on me, that although Lenie Cohen-Nijstad was clearly visible as one of the Fliegende Kolonne, she was only seen in the first one and a half minutes of the film.

That part contains the pictures of people disembarking at Westerbork from a train which has come from Amsterdam. In the following nine minutes of the film, in which the outgoing transport to Auschwitz and Bergen-Belsen can be seen, there are other young women from the Fliegende Kolonne going about their work, but Mrs Cohen is not amongst them.

So she had not been on the Westerbork platform that day. On 19 May 1944, she had been working as a cleaner in Port Natal in Assen, as she had already informed me. And so she was not in the film shots of the departure of the train.

When I put down the phone, I decided to reopen my search; I knew now that in order to continue to search for the identity of the girl in the door opening, I would have to turn to the Dutch Gypsy community.

But where were they and how could I approach them?

A study of the persecution of Gypsies in Holland between the years 1940-1945 has been published by Professor Ben Sijes of the Rijksinstituut voor Oorlogsdocumentatie, in collaboration with five Amsterdam history doctorate students.

It is a remarkable book, because thirty-five years after the deportation of Gypsies from Westerbork, it makes the first attempt to give a full description of what happened to Dutch Gypsies in the Second World War. Ben Sijes, who at that time was even more conscientious about the role of the Oorlogsdocumentatie than the director Lou de Jong, realised in 1979 that although so many years had passed since the Liberation, there was still hardly any information available about the murder of the Gypsies of the Netherlands. Even in 1955 nothing was mentioned under the entry *"Zigeuners"* in any Dutch encyclopedia about the persecution of the Gypsies by the Nazis. The reason? According to Sijes the raid of 16th May 1944 and the deportation of Gypsies three days later had taken place almost unnoticed. And in Camp Westerbork the number of deported Gypsies, 245, was submerged beneath that of the many thousands of Jewish victims taken from the camp by train over a two year period.

Sijes believed that another reason for overlooking the Gypsy persecution was the scant interest the Dutch had in "those people," dreaded because of their "thieving lightfingers." Not one word about the persecution of the Gypsies was to be found in Dutch encyclopedias, although they did mention the Gypsies' "typical mind set of tricks and deception" and "low moral code". That this view still held good in post-war Holland was shown by the fact that not one single Dutchman or German had been condemned for participating in the expulsion and death of the Dutch Gypsies.

In the middle of January I took up Sijes' book, which I had glanced at fleetingly, and to be honest, without much real interest, after its publication in 1979. I now concentrated on the footnotes which gave the source of the researchers' information.

At the end of the last chapter I read, "Of the roughly 245 Gypsies forcibly removed from Holland, as far as it is known, 30 returned to Holland, probably 16 women and 14 men." The footnote stated: "Facts supplied by the Information Bureau of the Dutch Red Cross."

From an earlier part of the book it was clear to me that Sijes' research team had spoken to a number of the returned Gypsies. The reports of these interviews would probably be found in one of the many cabinets in the Rijksinstituut voor Oorlogsdocumentatie. I could go and look for them, note the names of the survivors and check if they were still alive almost fifty years after having escaped being gassed in Auschwitz.

But there was something that held me back from knocking on the doors of the Oorlogsdocumentatie. I was frightened that I would have to explain my precise reason for searching in the Gypsy archives. Now that I finally found myself on the trail of the girl between the wagon doors, I was getting a bit paranoid. If by any chance, word got out that the girl in the Westerbork film was a little Gypsy child, I had no doubt that someone would use that knowledge before I had had a chance to follow it up, and offer this scrap of information to the evening news programme *Nova*, or to another television current affairs slot, where it would be discussed at great length.

So I wouldn't go to the Rijksinstituut for War Documents. But how, after so many years, could I find Gypsies who had travelled on the train of 19th May 1944, returned after the war, and perhaps knew who the girl was?

One afternoon I sat in my newspaper office, thinking things over, when my glance strayed to the empty desk on my left. Daan Overhoff, my friend and colleague, had sat there for almost two years, before dying young and leaving me with many warm memories. One of my most cherished memories was his noisy manner of working. Daan, after a long and almost autistic relationship with his word processor, would always inform us that the piece of work he had just finished was, like each of his pieces, the *chef d'oeuvre* of his twenty-five years in journalism. Then everyone in the office, busy or not with their own journalistic high point, had their concentration broken for a few minutes by Daan's repeated cries of "Hear, hear!"

Suddenly I saw Daan sitting there, his chair tilted back, keyboard pushed away, hands clapping above his head, his long legs on the desk. "Merry is the Gypsy life!" he cried. "But now forget that and read all about it! Next Saturday in this paper; the Gypsy is born out of necessity, we gave him his name and then stood by when he was killed in the war!"

I often have this sort of vivid recollection. This one was particularly appropriate: I thanked Daan's spirit and phoned our document department. "A couple of years ago my late colleague Overhoff wrote a piece about Gypsies. Can you send me a copy?"

A few minutes later I was looking at Daan's article of 13th October 1990. The headline was, "The Gypsy is born out of necessity." The caption read: "Dr Leo Lucassen complains about government prejudice."

The article covered the thesis of the young historian Lucassen who, following Sijes' study, had spent several years researching further into the history of Dutch Gypsies.

A few days later I had Lucassen's dissertation before me, *En men noemde hen zigeuners...* (A people called Gypsies). It described the history of the Kalderash, Ursari, Lovari and Sinti in Holland during the period 1750 — 1944.

I opened Chapter 1 and saw that it began with a quotation in small print:

"When we were picked up, there were no Germans to be seen. My father was woken early by someone knocking at the door. He opened the door and found loads of Dutch police officers standing there. And on the opposite side of the street, across the water near the brewery, they'd already pulled a lot of people out of their houses. Our street was the last. Then the Dutch police came and dragged us from our houses. We all had to go with them to the police station. Only on arrival in Westerbork did we see any Germans. The Dutch police who were with us handed us over and they gave some sort of book to a high-up German soldier. There were all sort of things about us in it, how many people there were and so on. We were shaved bald one by one, and we had to wash. And on the third day we still thought we could go home, but then they pushed us into cattlewagons and we had to go to Auschwitz."

In the notes at the end of the book I saw that the quotation came from a book by Jan Beckers: *Me hum Sinthu* (I am a Sinti). *Gesprekken met Zigeuners over de vervolging in de periode '40-45 en de jaren daarna* (Conversations with Gypsies about their persecution in the period 1940-50 and the following years).

I spent an hour on the telephone trying to locate Jan Beckers. He lived in Vlissingen in the southwestern province of Zeeland. I left a message on his answering machine saying that I urgently needed to see him. Would he phone me back as quickly as possible?

Jan Beckers did so in the late evening, sounding cheerful and friendly. I introduced myself and said I was researching the Westerbork transport of 19 May 1944 which had taken a group of Gypsies to Auschwitz. I told him that I had a scholarly work before me which began with a few paragraphs from his book.

The man from Vlissingen didn't know about the quotation but said he felt very honoured. "That's just an old book of mine," he said, "from 1980 or so. What quote did they use in the thesis?"

I read it out.

"Those are Crasa's words," Jan Beckers told me, "she was sent to Auschwitz when she was fifteen or sixteen.

With the train from Westerbork, that's right."

"Crasa?"

"Crasa Wagner. In the Register of Births and Deaths she's registered as Theresia Wagner, but Crasa is her Gypsy name."

"Is Crasa still alive?"

"Sure," said Jan Beckers, "and as far as I know she still lives in the place where I spoke to her years ago; the caravan park of Spijkenisse."

Chapter 13

Settela

Having felt depressed all weekend, I reported to work on Monday 7th February 1994. Later that morning I attended a meeting about the contents of the coming Saturday supplement. But I was so lethargic and absentminded I didn't have much to contribute. I had spent most of Saturday and Sunday in my room, sometimes reading notes but mainly staring out of the window. I felt frustrated and also like a prisoner. I had to be patient and wait till the weekend, which was when, according to Jan Beckers, the Gypsies regularly met together, leaving their scattered camps to gather in the caravans where their parents lived.

But, as Beckers had reiterated in our subsequent conversations — particularly after consulting his Limburg friend Roger, even more at home in the world of the Gypsies than Beckers — "if you suddenly appear amongst the Gypsies it will lead to the opposite of what you want. That won't open any doors for you but will shut them for good. Just wait," Jan Beckers suggested, "till Roger and I have explored the matter further and then we can introduce you, have patience."

As our editorial meeting ended it seemed to me that I was faced with a Monday afternoon in which I had nothing particular to do. I decided to do what I could not leave undone, and said to René van Zanten, chief of our team of reporters: "If you don't mind, I'd like to go to Spijkenisse this afternoon."

Van Zanten understood what I had in mind. I had bent his ear often enough about the girl and he knew I was convinced she was a Gypsy. Moreover a week earlier he had given me his own copy of Jan Beckers' book, *Me hum Sinthu,* about which he, coincidently, had written a piece in 1980. "Go to Spijkenisse," he said. "That's what I'd do."

91

I was very nervous on the way to Spijkenisse. Emerging from the Beneluxtunnel at Pernis near Rotterdam, I drove along the former island of Putten under a damp leaden sky. Near Hoogvliet, some kilometers before Spijkenisse, I wanted to turn around and drive home. I was sure I was heading for disaster; as soon as I arrived, I'd be thrown out of the camp as an intruder. Had I never heard of the respect that should be shown to an old Gypsy mama, especially a lady like Crasa Wagner who had suffered so much from other intruders and raiders fifty years ago? Clear off!

But all the same I drove to the Groene Kruisweg, over the Oude Maas bridge, and took the left turning to the area of Groenoord where Crasa's camp was situated. Not far from the river, there is a country backwater with non-descript warehouses, where criminals can hide kidnapped industrialists for weeks on end, make porno films, or where bets can be placed on pitbull fights. Near the spot where the deserted road enters a no man's land, stands the showroom of a car dealer. I drew up outside the building, and reconsidered my position. Three hundred metres away I could see the Spijkenisse caravan centre; obviously the Municipality could not have found anywhere further from civilisation to make into a caravan park. Taking a deep breath I headed towards it.

The paved road wound in an S through the caravan park past large fixed mobile homes with cars parked in front of them, many of them Mercedes, and racks on which laundry was drying. Halfway along, I came across a group of men having a heated discussion next to a small freight lorry. I stopped next to them, opened my window and asked timidly if they knew where Mrs Theresia Wagner lived.

"Second wagon over there, near the rubbish bin," said a man with a disfigured face, who was standing nearest to my car. The men paid me no further attention — as if every Monday afternoon some guy from town came for Mrs Wagner — and continued their quarrel. Surprised, I wondered what had happened to the famous typical Gypsy social control which could not be breached by outsiders.

I pulled up next to the rubbish container, got out and went to the caravan which had been pointed out to me. I was holding the book, *Me hum Sinthu,* with the cover exposed. I hadn't really thought about this, but it helped; a small window opened next to the steps by the caravan door. An old man with a white beard stuck out his head, looked at me, then at the book and said; "I already understand, come on up."

He opened the door and I went into a room of about four by eight metres, bordered by large windows partly darkened by dozens of dolls, big ones and small ones, most of them beautifully dressed. The caravan was extremely tidy and everything seemed to have just been cleaned and polished. To the left of the entrance, near the stove, sat an old woman on a low chair, with her legs drawn up beneath her so I could not tell how tall she was.

The man with the white beard went to sit in a chair next to the television, facing the street. He said nothing. Nor did the woman; she just looked from the book that I was now holding firmly like some sort of letter of recommendation, to gaze up into my face. I stood awkwardly and we were all silent for a little while. Then I said: "Good day, Mrs Wagner; you are Crasa Wagner?"

She had a full round face with deep creases running from her nose to her chin. There were traces of black in her grey hair. Her deepset eyes were dark and somewhat shy. She gestured to me to sit on the settee opposite her.

"Yes, I am Crasa."

I began to speak slowly and clearly, as if to a lip reader. I don't know why. I told her that I had spent a long time looking into the circumstances under which, on 19th May 1944, a group of Dutch Gypsies had been transported from Westerbork to Auschwitz. And that I knew that she, Crasa Wagner, a sixteen-year old girl at the time, had been one of them, transported in a goods wagon, and that in Auschwitz her father and mother, and all her brothers

93

and sisters, apart from one male child, had been murdered.

The woman interrupted me; she sighed and seemed to rouse herself. "I know that well enough," she said in a flat voice. She drew her legs up higher. "I get distraught about it every day, I was recently in hospital again because of it. I am always frightened, especially now that the Wall has come down in Germany. Because now the Nazis can come again from the east. I ask all the Gypsies that come here from abroad what is going on over there. Only last week I had a similar conversation with someone, a man who had come from that country in the east where there is now war."

She fell silent and I was able to continue. A film was made of the transport from Westerbork on 19th May 1944, I said, and during the filming the camera briefly pointed at one of the children from the Gypsy group. I took from my wallet the eight by twelve centimetre photograph I'd been carrying around for almost a year; the photograph of the girl with the headcloth in the door opening of the train wagon.

I laid it on the low table between Crasa and me. The old man (Crasa's husband, known as Ome Gerrit [uncle Gerrit], I learned later) stood up, took the photo, looked at it, shrugged his shoulders and gave it to his wife. She held it about a metre from her eyes.

"That is one of the Steinbach children," she said at once.

My heart thudded. I felt the veins in my temple stand out.

"She was killed in Auschwitz," Crasa continued and gave me back the photo. "Her father stayed behind in Holland and died of grief after the war."

My head spun. Could it really be that on a Monday afternoon in Spijkenisse, not even ten minutes after visiting the first survivor I had found from the Westerbork Gypsy transport, the girl who for almost half a century had been known throughout the world as the anonymous victim of the deportations, had been given back her surname? "The girl is standing in the opening of a train wagon," I said. "The photo, the film shot, is world famous; how could it be that you, Crasa Wagner, have never mentioned to anyone that the girl was one of the Steinbachs?"

"Because no one ever has asked me."

And calmly, the exact opposite of what I was feeling, she related: "I was with the girl in the wagon. I sat on the floor behind her and she stood there at the front, near the door. Her mother cried out that she must get away from the door. Because we could hear the doors being bolted shut on the outside. 'Get away from there,' her mother cried, 'otherwise your head will get stuck!' I ought to know the child's forename, because her mother cried it out while she was so angry and frightened: 'Ssst, ssst, get away from there!'"

Crasa thought deeply, her head bowed. "I can't remember it."

Silence. I held my breath.

"No. But I must know it, the forename. I have seen that photo of yours many times, on the television. And my daughter once said to me, 'That looks like you as a young girl.' But I said, 'No, that is...' No, now I can't remember her first name, but she was one of the Steinbach children."

A couple of minutes passed during which I didn't dare say anything. I could see Crasa delving into the depths of her memory and didn't want to disturb her. "I believe," she said, almost mumbling, "that she was looking at a dog which was walking along outside the train. It was a light coloured dog, quite large. Her mother moved her away from the door at the last moment."

Crasa Wagner looked at me tiredly, somewhat reproachfully. "She is dead, you know, that child," she said. "She was too young to work in Auschwitz. She was about eleven, they only wanted strong children like me. In Auschwitz, I was put to work paving streets."

Ome Gerrit, who had been sitting immobile next to his wife, looking at her with an almost devoted expression, now joined in the conversation. That gave me a breathing space to calm myself down and think about what tactics I needed to question this woman I had only just met and might never meet again, who had sat only one and a half metres from the girl in the door opening of the wagon train, as close as I was now sitting to her.

Ome Gerrit told me that his wife was still searching for the relatives she had had to leave behind when she was sent on to Ravensbrück some weeks after her arrival in Auschwitz. A couple of years ago she had asked someone to write a letter on her behalf to the television programme, *Spoorloos* (Without Trace).

"Then we got a report back that they would take a look at the subject," said the old man, "but we never heard anything more." Ome Gerrit spat out a sentence; "The television called it a subject! A subject!"

Crasa joined in the conversation again. She said: "My father and mother and us eight kids were taken from The Hague to Westerbork and then by train to Auschwitz. There I was reunited with my two older sisters who had got married in Germany. My mother went into the ovens with the other children, but those two sisters and another one were able to get away. But perhaps I dreamed it all — do you know when Auschwitz was liberated?"

I said I believed it was early in 1945, in January. I promised to look up the exact date at home and telephone her.

We passed the next quarter of an hour with many silences and some bursts of memory. Every now and then, little by little, Crasa described how she had spent the morning of her departure from Westerbork with her family in a huge barrack. They were given bread and someone brought small buckets to use for defecating into on the train.

"The Steinbachs were a large family and they sat near us. The mother of that girl had an unfortunate little boy. He was lame, she always carried him on her back. The Steinbachs were really old-fashioned Gypsies. I first saw

96

them in the encampment in Susteren in Zuid-Limburg. That's where we went in 1938 when we came to Holland, when we fled from the Germans. The Steinbach family also had a great great grandmother, an *Urgrossmutter* — the woman was well over a hundred and she shoved herself around the camp on her bottom."

Crasa said that she had arrived at Auschwitz on 21 May 1944. "We saw a lot of smoke coming from a chimney. They said that it was bedclothes burning but we knew soon enough that the smoke from the pipe came from human flesh. A young lad said to me a couple of weeks later, 'My mother went through the pipe yesterday.' Then I knew."

She asked if she could see the photo of the girl once more. I handed it to her and she looked at it again. "I said her name out loud once," she said, "when I said to my daughter: 'That is so and so Steinbach!' But what was it now? Dina? Sofia?"

I asked Crasa whether the girl's headcloth meant anything to her.

"That was a bit of cloth or pillowcase," she said matter of factly. "We all had something like that on our heads. We all picked up a piece of cloth when our heads were shaved. My mother gave me a pillowcase. Because I had to cover that bald head of mine. Our hair was our greatest glory, our thick long black hair — we all had it, such a beautiful head of hair. But my cloth didn't stay on properly. The thing kept falling off."

Crasa Wagner turned in on herself again. She fell silent and stared at the floor. Ome Gerrit went into a corner to rummage for the letter from the editor of the programme, *Spoorloos* about the "subject." But he couldn't find the piece of paper. Then he asked me to take down the telephone number of the caravan so I could phone them later when I had found out when Auschwitz was liberated. But Ome Gerrit didn't know the dialing code of Spijkenisse and he turned to consult his motionless wife, just as the old Gypsy woman suddenly straightened her legs and sat bolt upright.

Her eyes were huge. It seemed as if the folds on her dark face had disappeared.

"Settela!" she cried.

"That was her name: Settela! Her mother yelled: 'Settela, get away from the door, or your head will get stuck!' Settela!"

Settela Steinbach — it was Monday afternoon 7th February 1994, five to four. The girl had got her name back.

In the evening I opened my personal computer and once more called up the file, "Esther", to which I had added so many documents over the last twelve months. I renamed it — Settela.

But the quest was not yet over.

Chapter 14

Stein

After Holland was liberated from the Germans in May 1945, and the Japanese Occupation of the Dutch East Indies ended in the August of that year, the establishment of War Graves and Fields of Honour was immediately begun, initially throughout Europe, and subsequently in Asia.

It was not possible to give all the victims of the World War a final and dignified resting place. There are many hundreds of thousands who were lost without trace or whose remains were destroyed. This was the fate, for example, of members of the armed forces who were reported missing or drowned at sea. An even greater number of those whose last resting place is unknown is made up of the victims of persecution who were thrown into mass graves, and particularly those who lost their lives in the German extermination camps, mainly through being gassed, whose bodies were then burnt in crematoria.

In Holland, a way has been found to keep alive the memory of this large group of war victims without graves. With the help of many institutions, particularly the Red Cross, their names have been collected from international registers and inscribed in forty-two War Graves' Foundation *Books of Remembrance*. These books were compiled over a period of about twenty-five years, initially with manual typeset, in an edition of twelve printings. A complete set of these books lies in the chapel of the Field of Honour in Loenen on the Veluwe in east Holland. Parts 4 to 33, containing the names of over one hundred thousand Jews who were deported from Holland and subsequently murdered, are to be found in Yad Vashem, the Israeli Institute in Jerusalem for the commemoration of Jewish martyrs.

In part 2 of the *Books of Remembrance*, are the names of Dutch non-Jews who were taken to the camps of Auschwitz, Buchenwald, Grosz-Rosen, Lublin, Mittelbau, Ravensbrück, Sachsenhausen, Sobibor, Stutthof, Theresienstadt and Warsaw.

On pages 81, 82 and 83 of this particular section, the name Steinbach appears twenty-six times as the surname of people who lost their lives in Auschwitz, Germany or Central Europe in 1944 and 1945 or, in four cases, are reported missing.

I copied the names of the twenty-six Steinbachs, grouped them into male and female, and placed them in order of birth, with their place of birth, age on 19th May 1944 and the place where they died.

There are seventeen female Steinbachs:

> Theresia, 14-6-1899, Wettringen, 45; Auschwitz.
> Emilia, 23-3-1902, Antwerp, 42; Auschwitz.
> Maria, 6-11-1912, Hoensbroek, 31; missing.
> Anna, 24-3-1916, Lengenszala, 28; Auschwitz.
> Labora, 9-7-1918, Noord-Scharwoude, 26; missing.
> Magdalena Gertruda, 14-9-1922, Brunssum, 22; missing.
> Jozefina, 7-12-1923, Eindhoven, 20½; Auschwitz.
> Anna Maria, 11-5-1926 Kerkrade, 18; Auschwitz.
> Elisabeth, 14-11-1926, Meerssen, 17½; Central Europe.
> Johanna Cornelia, 18-3-1930, Maastricht, 14; Central Europe.
> Walda, 12-5-1930, Keulen, 14; Auschwitz.
> Anna Maria, 23-12-1934, Born, 9½; Auschwitz.
> Florentina Maria, 14-9-1937, Sittard, 7; Auschwitz.
> Anna Maria, 15-6-1942, Linne, 2; Auschwitz.
> Sophia, 26-10-1942, Eindhoven, over 1½; missing.
> Anna, 11-2-1943, Roermond, 15 months; Auschwitz.
> Johanna, 6-4-1944, Eindhoven, 1½ months; Auschwitz.

The names of nine male Steinbachs appear in the *Book of Remembrance:*

> Friedrich, 30-12-1883, Amsterdam, 59; Auschwitz.
> Karel, 22-10-1893, Dinxperlo, 50; missing.

Friedrich, 20-6-1918, Sittard, 24; Germany.
Willem-Hendrik, 19-2-1925, Brunssum, 19; Ellrich-
   Nordhausen.
Celestinus, 13-2-1929, Heerlen, 14; Auschwitz.
Philibert, 4-9-1932, Geleen, 11½; Auschwitz.
Johannes Antonius, 27-12-1932, Brunssum; missing.
Willem, 28-8-1939, Sittard, just over 4½; Auschwitz.
Henricus, 14-9-1942, Horn, 1½; Auschwitz.

A week after Crasa Wagner had mentioned the name of
Settela Steinbach to me, I went to Limburg with the list of
the twenty-six Steinbachs. This province, the birthplace of
most of the Steinbachs who had been murdered in the
camps, was home to another survivor from the Gypsy
transport of 19th May 1944. This was Magdalena Berger,
who as a fifteen year old girl, had lived, like Crasa Wagner,
in one of the small houses in the slums of the
Bilderdijkstraat and near the Veenkade in The Hague.

I had meanwhile learnt that Settela was a Gypsy forename. The name by which the child had been recorded in
the official register was quite possibly a competely different one, an everyday or Christian name.

In Crasa Wagner's memory, Settela had been roughly
eleven years old when she had left Westerbork on the
train. There were only three names in that age range on
the list of dead and missing Steinbachs; Johanna Cornelia,
who was fourteen, Walda, also fourteen, and Anna Maria,
nine and a half years old.

Which of these girls had been called Settela?

It was freezing hard as I drove through the province of
Limburg. It was minus 10 or 12 degrees and a stiff wind
was blowing on this coldest day of the winter.

I had to get to Stein, on the Julianakanaal in the south
of Limburg, where the caravans of Magdalena Berger and
her family were apparently located. The centre of Stein
was dead; it was the Monday morning of Carnival Week
and everyone was either sleeping or sheltering from the
cold. As I drove past a shopping centre I saw a man out

walking his dog. One of his eyes was trembling with cold and an icycle hung from his nose — something you rarely see in Holland.

The man informed me that there were three caravan parks in the village. The Veestraat camp was nearby — to get there I would have to turn back a little way, towards the motorway. Apologetically he said that he was too cold to stand still any longer to explain how to reach the two other Gypsy camps in Stein. Man and dog walked away.

I drove around and found Veestraat. In front of the slope of a typical ancient Limburg earth wall, a narrow road wound between frosty meadows. I drove past the back of a rectangular low wooden bungalow which gleamed with paint, and thought; it's too chic here for a municipal caravan park. But when I turned right, I found myself in a little square between another section of about ten similar bungalows, and realised from the steps near the doors that they were huge mobile homes. Nothing moved on the small square.

I got out and banged on the door of the nearest mobile home to escape from the harsh biting wind. A tall woman in her sixties appeared at the door, looking at me with a mixture of surprise and pity in her beautiful dark eyes when she saw how cold I was — I wasn't even wearing an overcoat. Without asking who I was, she invited me to come in quickly. I went in, the door closed fast behind me and I stepped onto a soft carpet next to a table made of heavy dark brown wood measuring at least six meters, which dominated the caravan.

The woman was goodlooking and the complexion of her proud face was youthful and perfect. There was no trace of grey in her thick black hair, which was tied back with a lace. Her long dark-blue blouse patterned with white dots fell right over her skirt. Her forearms were bare and on the left one I saw a tattoed number prefaced by a Z.

I said cautiously, in a tone tinged with guilt, that I was searching for a lady, Magdalena Berger, who lived in a caravan park in Stein.

102

"That is my name."

I gave a start and was lost for words. Then I introduced myself and asked if she was the Magdalena Berger who had been taken by train from Westerbork to Auschwitz as a young girl in 1944.

Now she gave a start and I could see that she regretted letting me in. But she answered, yes, she had been in Westerbork and Auschwitz. She preferred not to talk about it. And really, she could not remember anything about it.

Neither of us knew what to do in this awkward situation, alone in the huge caravan. "Would you like a cup of coffee?" asked Magdalena Berger finally.

She gestured me to sit at the long table and took the seat opposite mine. I took the photo of the girl in the door opening from my inside pocket and lay it on the table in front of Magdalena Berger.

"This child was with you in the train from Westerbork. She was called Settela Steinbach. Did you know her?"

She looked fleetingly at the photo. "I do not know her," she said. "I believe that I have seen the photo a few times, but I know nothing about that time any more. Steinbach...?" She looked at me reproachfully, but was too goodnatured to show me to the door.

We were silent for a moment; I drank my sweet milky coffee and Magdalena Berger sighed. She rested her left arm with its Auschwitz tattoo before me on the table. I dared not ask anything else, it was better that I went.

Then the telephone rang in the corner of the huge caravan. Magdalena Berger went over to it and began to speak quickly in a language unintelligible to me. But because what she was saying sounded affirmative and explanatory, and she nodded in my direction a couple of times, I guessed that the call was from someone in the camp and that she was reassuring the person on the other end of the line: yes, an outsider had come to see her and no, there was nothing to fear.

Nevertheless, just one a half minutes after Magdalena Berger had put down the receiver, the door of

103

the caravan swung open, letting in a gust of cold air, and in came a man who turned out to be Magdalena's husband; Willem Rosenberg, about seventy, heavyset, jaunty, and extremely friendly. His only outer garment was a heavy cardigan, so presumably he had come from somewhere nearby in the camp. His wife had evidently told him on the phone in her rapid tongue who I was and why I had come, because immediately after Rosenberg had shaken my hand, he grasped the photo on the table and picked it up.

"I recognise her," he said at once, "she's been on the television many times, that girl."

I said; "Mrs Crasa Wagner in Spijkenisse told me that her name is Settela and she was one of the Steinbach children."

William Rosenberg remained motionless. His eyes roved a few times from me to the photo in his hand. "Settela," he cried, "of course; Settela! I knew her. I knew her whole family; she was one of Moeselman's children. They are dead, they all died in the war, Moeselman's children. And he himself is dead, but that was after the war."

Rosenberg came over and sat at the table opposite me, next to his wife Magdalena — Berger, I now realised, being her maiden name. Magdalena looked at the photo of Settela in Willem's hand again. She shrugged her shoulders. "I don't know any more."

I tried to refresh her memory: "According to Crasa, the girl in the train had a brother with lame legs. His mother always carried him on her back."

Now Magdalena's eyes lit up. "No!" she said, "that lad had another mother; she was also a Steinbach. That one had a lame little boy. His legs were always crossed behind him under his bottom."

She thought very deeply.

"That child was called Tikono," she said.

Willem Rosenberg looked at his wife proudly. In the meantime, he too had remembered something. "Settela was Moeselman's daughter and Tikono was the son of

Koleman, Moeselman's brother. Koleman's still alive, he lives in Gulpen or Valkenburg, I believe he's ninety... But you can't speak to him, see, he's much too old for that."

Should I go or should I stay? Was it fitting to act as I did, barging into people's houses unannounced and showing them a photo which dragged them back half a century to a time when they had been persecuted and murdered? I looked again at the camp number with the Z for *Zigeuner* on Magdalena's forearm, then I took the photo of Settela from Rosenberg's strong hand and looked once more at the childish face with the headcloth. I decided to stay longer.

Magdalena had stood up and was now busying herself at the large stove. Willem Rosenberg said to me conspiratorially, in a soft and loving tone, that I should not pay attention to his wife or talk to her any more. She didn't want to remember the war. It wasn't so bad for him, as he had not endured what his wife had; the camps, Auschwitz, Ravensbrück and more — she used to talk about it sometimes, but a long time had passed since she had done so.

Willem Rosenberg told me that as a young man, he had hidden when the Germans began to round up the Gypsies. But now, if I didn't mind him asking, he had a question for me; what was Settela, that girl in the photo, to do with me; why had I come all the way from The Hague to Zuid-Limburg today in this terrible cold?

Just as I was about to tell him about my long search, the caravan door opened and in came a lovely young woman with bare feet. Although she had only walked a short way from one caravan to the other, she shivered in her short dress and woollen shawl. She was the exact image of the Gypsy girl in the painting which hangs above so many Dutch sideboards. She rattled off something to Willem and Magdalena in her language, whilst throwing questioning glances in my direction, and finally, under obvious instructions from the old man and woman, gave me a radiant smile and stuck out her small light-brown hand with its ring covered fingers.

105

"My daughter," said Willem Rosenberg.

She turned out to be the first of a series of children living in the camp, grandchildren and other relatives, who now began to drop in to visit Willem (Gypsy name Hokelo, I was later to learn, but the children called him Tata), and Magdalena (who was addressed as Atta). By noon I was sitting round the table with almost twenty Gypsies of all ages, each more beautiful than the next. The small photograph of Settela was passed from hand to hand as Willem Rosenberg related to his family, half in Dutch and half in his mother tongue, that this *meneer* (gentleman) from The Hague had discovered that the girl in the train was one of them; a Gypsy child who, during the war, had been sent from Westerbork to Auschwitz to be killed. I could tell that expressions of surprise and horror were being exchanged around the circle, although I could not understand the words. Mother and grandma Magdalena Berger stood by the stove stirring an enormous shining pan of bean soup while her children and grandchildren talked. She took no further part in the conversation, only coming to the table to exchange full ashtrays for empty ones. Young and old smoked heavily.

The stream of visitors had still not stopped. The caravan door opened again for the umpteenth time and Tony Weiss came in. He was not a relative, but a friend of the Rosenbergs who often dropped round on Mondays. A neat man of seventy, he had a dark face with deep set eyes behind lightly tinted glasses, and wore a leather jacket. Toni Weiss was to prove to be a great source of knowledge about the past.

Weiss, I learned from the others round the table, was a real Gypsy, but since marrying a "white" woman a few years ago, he now lived in a council house in Stein. Toni Weiss was very eloquent and well-informed. Had he not told me that he was illiterate, I would doubtlessly have described him as a very well-read man.

106

Weiss picked up the photo of the girl from the table and held it up. Was I saying that this child was called Settela? Well, then I was right.

"Sure I know her," said Toni Weiss, "Settela, one of Moeselman's little girls. Her mother was called Toetela. Of course this is Settela, this girl in the photo. Now I know for certain — if what you say is true; this is a photo from the Gypsy train from Westerbork. I have often brooded over the photo when I've seen it on television. I knew that face — but it was always presented as if she were a little Jewish girl. No pictures have been kept of <u>our</u> people who disappeared during the war, as far as I know. I've always understood that the Gypsies disappeared without trace. But now I know; Settela, sure that is Settela! I knew her — and her brothers Elmo and Willy too. And Kali, her sister, and Mokkela, another of Settela's sisters."

Toni Weiss now understood why he had once said what he had to the son of one of the Steinbach's nephews. The man had two daughters, one of whom looked exactly like that girl in the famous photo. "I said to him, 'Frans, that looks just like one of your girls; that child they're always showing in the programmes about the war on TV!' So I wasn't really wrong, there was indeed a family likeness!"

Toni Weiss sat down. Everyone round the table, young and old, hung on his every word. Now and then Willem Rosenberg joined in as Toni Weiss told them what he knew about the Steinbach family, to which the child in the photo belonged. Sometimes the stories came slowly, one memory calling up another. I sat and listened for more than two hours, and sometimes I put a question but I never made a suggestion.

Moeselman and Toetela Steinbach were the parents of a large family with, Toni Weiss guessed, about eight or ten children. Moeselman had a younger brother, Koleman. Koleman was married to one of Toetela's older sisters.

One day during the war the SS, Grüne Polizei and the Dutch *Marechaussee* (Military Police) picked up Toetela and her sister — "could she have been called Boetela?" — in the large caravan camp where all the Gypsies had been obliged to stay, somewhere near Eindhoven. The two fathers, Moeselman and Koleman, were not in the camp at that time; they had been picked up earlier or had gone into hiding — just like Toni Weiss himself, who had taken refuge in a safe house in Sittard.

The two mothers and the Steinbach children were sent to the concentration camp, to Auschwitz and none of them — not Toetela or her sister nor any of the children — ever returned.

Moeselman, Settela's father, died of grief not long after the war, all alone in a caravan near Maastricht. After the liberation, he had done almost nothing other than seek, seek and seek till the day he died. Moeselman still thought that his wife and children would return; he had completely refurnished his caravan with beds and other items and had been waiting for them throughout the last weeks of his life. His brother Koleman had evidently accepted earlier the fact that his wife and four children had been gassed by the Nazis in the concentration camp.

But Moeselman had not. Understandably: he was renowned amongst all the other Limburg Gypsies for his almost exaggerated preoccupation with his family.

Toni Weiss gestured widely and said: "Moeselman always wanted to keep his wife and children together, so he could watch over them. In the winter, for example, when it was really cold, he took care that the little stove in their caravan didn't go out during the night."

Toni Weiss also remembered that Moeselman had been a fantastically good pianist and violinist. Before the war, people all over Limburg and on the other side of the German border had listened to him with great enjoyment. "He was a left handed violinist, like Elmo, his oldest son. Elmo also played beautifully — and, by the way, Willy was developing into a good violinist as well. Willy was a younger brother and I knew him the best. We were roughly the same age, and as a child I played with him and we mucked around together. Settela would have been about three or four years younger than Willy."

Toni Weiss had forgotten the time. As he looked at his watch and saw that it was already almost two o'clock, he gasped and said that his wife was waiting for him at home with some roast chicken; she would be really angry. Weiss was about to get up, but then something else seemed to flash into his mind. He switched into his own language and excitedly raised his voice to say something that sounded like an order. One of the young women got up quickly and went to the corner of the caravan to use the phone.

Then Toni Weiss said to me; "In his good times, in those years before the war, Moeselman often played with another Gypsy musician, an accordionist. That man is still alive and not so long ago he gave me a couple of photos that he'd kept as a keepsake of Moeselman and his family. But, well, what should I do with photos of people who aren't related to me? So I gave them to someone from the Steinbach family, to Kercheman, Rico's son. He was the third brother: Moeselman, Koleman, and then there was Rico."

Weiss said that Kercheman Steinbach had just been phoned with the urgent request to come at once to the Veestraat camp with the family photos Weiss had recently given him. If all was well, the man — "one of Settela's first cousins, *meneer*!" — would now be on his way to us.

Twenty minutes later Kercheman came in. With his trim bourgeois appearance, his close cut blond hair, neat jacket and shirt with a dull tie, he seemed a little out of place in the company of the beautiful Gypsies in the Rosenbergs' caravan.

Weiss introduced Kercheman to me and he greeted me with a hesitant handshake. He didn't quite get what was going on here.

109

Meanwhile, Toni Weiss had taken from Kercheman's left hand an envelope stamped with the logo of a medical insurance company, and was shaking the contents onto the table. Five small photos fell out, a little discoloured. They had been stuck onto light cardboard.

"Look," said Toni Weiss, "that was Moeselman. That was before the war, in his good times."

I saw a dark handsome man with a pointed nose and a little moustache, looking towards the camera in a self-assured manner. He was wearing a *borsalino*, one of those Italian swagger hats with a dent and broad rim. I turned the photo over. On the back of the cardboard was written in fine light-blue ballpoint: "Heinrich Steinbach, born in Gründorf, 11-11-1901."

"A first class violinist," Toni Weiss said, visibly moved. He lay another two photos of Heinrich Steinbach in front of me. "This is what he looked like after the war. That's when Moeselman must have sensed that his wife and children weren't coming back from the concentration camp."

Moeselman was now bareheaded with a thin face. His glance was vacant, his eyes were sunken and had dark circles beneath them; he looked seedy.

"Tragic, isn't it?" said Weiss.

He pushed the fourth photo towards me. "This was Toetela, Moeselman's wife and Settela's mother."

In the photo I saw a woman grasping a child who was hanging halfway across a chair to her left. It seemed to be a studio portrait. The woman was wearing a flower-patterned blouse and had placed a hand on her hip. She had medium length light-brown hair and radiant eyes.

I turned the photo over and read the thin lightblue ballpoint writing: "Emilia Steinbach, 23-3-1902."

Then Toni Weiss gave me the fifth and last photo. This was the identity photo of a fairhaired lad, whose sheepish look had been captured by the photographer. "Willy!" said Toni Weiss, "he was the mate I played with so often as a kid. Willy was one of Settela's older brothers."

Written on the back of Willy's photo was: "Celestinus Steinbach, 13-2-1929."

From my inside pocket, I took out the photocopies I'd made from the *Remembrance Book* of the War Graves' Foundation. These were the pages on which the name Steinbach appeared twenty-six times. I unfolded them and lay them next to the upturned photos on the table.

On page 81 it said: "Steinbach, Celestinus 13-2-1929 Heerlen 27-9-1944 Birkenau."

That was Willy, Settela's little brother.

On page 83, the fourth line read: "Steinbach-Steinbach, Emilia 23-3-1902 Antwerp Auschwitz."

Toetela, Settela's mother.

As I saw the names, first on the back of the photos in light ballpoint and then in the bold and solemn "Spectrum"-type of the *Remembrance Book*, I shivered.

Atta had finished preparing her bean soup and asked if I would like to eat with them. But I thanked her as politely and as aimiably as I could. I had spent more than three hours in the caravan, and felt exhausted.

Kercheman snatched back his photos, put them in the envelope and disappeared from the caravan, looking, I thought, a little angry.

Toni Weiss was sure that he was now too late for his roast chicken, so he remained to eat some soup.

I left Stein and drove out of Zuid-Limburg, the place where I had come so close to Settela's previous life.

But how Settela, the girl in the door opening of the wagon, had been entered in the Registrar of Births and Deaths, was still not established.

Chapter 15

Westerbork, 19 May 1944 —
Auschwitz, 31 July, 1st August 1944

"Lagerabschnitt BII"

May 1944 had started beautifully, with temperatures sometimes as high as in summer. On 14th May however, the weather broke and a bleak, changeable period followed. But on 19 May, the Friday after Ascension Day, the lovely spring weather returned. It was cloudless and dry with little wind, and although at dawn the temperature was just above zero, it reached 16°C by the afternoon.

At one o'clock on Friday afternoon, for the eighty-eighth time since 15 July 1942, a train left Westerbork bound for concentration camps in Germany and Poland. The transport left later than planned, delayed by the late arrival of the locomotive needed to pull the twenty or so wagons.

The long train comprised of three sections. In the first, which was made up of third-class passenger compartments, there were 238 people on their way to the camp of Bergen-Belsen. The rest of the train, with Auschwitz as its destination, was made up of coupled cattle and goods wagons, each one numbered with chalk figures.

The first of these wagons transported 208 Jewish prisoners, while Dutch Gypsies were locked into the rear section, which had been coupled to the train at the last moment. These Gypsies were 245 of the 578 who had been brought to Camp Westerbork from various places in Holland after the roundups of 16 and 17 May.

There were seventy-five people in the wagon with the chalked number 16.

Initially there had been seventy-four Gypsies in their family groups, but at the last minute someone else had been added. A man from the Ordnungsdienst who had supervised the boarding and closed the doors, wiped out the number "74 Pers" and replaced it with "75 Pers".

Amongst the seventy-five Gypsies were Theresia and Emilia Steinbach and thirteen of their children. Theresia, who was called Bütta, was at forty-four, the oldest of the mothers. She had three sons with her, Karl, Johannes and Jean, fifteen, eleven and ten respectively, and her fourteen year old daughter Walda.

Forty-two year old Emilia, whose Gypsy name was Toetela, was in the wagon with nine of her ten children; Willem-Hendrik, nineteen; Elisabeth, seventeen; Celestinus, fifteen; Johanna Cornelia, fourteen; Philibert, eleven; Anna Maria, nine; Florentina Maria, seven; Willem, four, and Anna Maria who was two.

Magdalena Gertruda, who at just under twenty was Emilia's oldest child, was not there. But this young woman, whose Gypsy name was Moekela, had not been part of Moeselman and Toetela Steinbach's family group since 1943.

Moekela had chosen to lead her own life, travelling with another Gypsy family through Belgium. Unknown to Toetela, her oldest child had been rounded up by the Germans in a raid on Belgian Gypsies at the beginning of 1944. On the 15th January she had been sent to Auschwitz-Birkenau in transport number 50 from the Belgian city of Mechelen.

Moekela, who had the number Z9781 tattoed on her arm, was killed in Birkenau on 5th April.

Bütta and Toetela and their thirteen children arrived in Westerbork on 16th May. On that Tuesday morning they had been woken very early in their little encampment near Eindhoven, by screams and people banging on the caravans. Following the travel restrictions imposed in the summer of 1943, their camp had become one of the central camps for Gypsies and caravan dwellers.

The police agents and *Landwachters* (paramilitary NSB-volunteers) who carried out the raids, had a list of Gypsies living in the Eindhoven camp. In the end, twenty-one families, including those of Bütta and Toetela, were driven out of the camp to Eindhoven railway station. There they had to get into a passenger train going first to the town of Den Bosch — where another thirty-nine Gypsies were taken aboard — and then travelling northwards. At about four in the afternoon their journey came to an end at Camp Westerbork.

Unlike most of the other Gypsy women, the two Steinbach sisters found themselves without the support of their husbands. Koleman and Moeselman had been arrested in Eindhoven a week earlier with their brother Rico and another four adult male Gypsies, and taken to the Amersfoort concentration camp.

The fifteen members of Theresa and Emilia Steinbach's family were amongst the large group of 578 people who had been brought from all over Holland to the Westerbork camp on 16 and 17 May. But more than half that number were quickly freed, mainly because it turned out that they were simply caravan dwellers, rather than Gypsies. On Thursday 19 May, Ascension Day, there were still 245 Gypsies in Westerbork; 29 adult males and 38 adult women, 68 boys and girls from sixteen to twenty-one, and 110 children under sixteen; they were chiefly members of Sinti families.

The Gypsies were enclosed in barrack 69, to the left of the Juden Durchgangslager Westerbork, where a small camp ringed by barbed wire was used for punishment and quarantine. For food, the Gypsies were given rotten potatoes, carrots and watery soup.

Before they could go into the barrack, they were examined by a doctor. They were deloused and had their heads shaved by other prisoners, a process which took one evening and one night and which greatly aroused the interest of the SS guards. The camp commandant himself, Obersturmführer Gemmeker, came to take a look towards morning, drunk and accompanied by several women.

114

Gemmeker said to a Jewish doctor who was examining the Gypsies, *"Na, Herr Doktor, das sind doch ganz andere Leute als Sie und ich, was?"* — (Well, *Herr Doktor*, these people are completely different from you and me, aren't they?)

When the Gypsies were forced into goods and cattle wagons on Friday morning, 19 May, all their baggage was disinfected. Even the violins that they had with them, twenty-seven in number, received this treatment.

Two of the violins in wagon 16 formed part of the luggage of Toetela Steinbach's oldest son, Willem-Hendrik, (Gypsy name Elmo), and his younger brother, Celestinus, who was called Willy.

On 22 May the train with 208 Jews and 245 Gypsies arrived at Auschwitz. Some of the Jews were sent to the gas chambers immediately after being examined on the platform by SS doctors. The group of 245 Gypsies went to Lagerabschnitt B II. This was the barrack section of Auschwitz-II in Birkenau, allocated to Gypsies and where a large group of Czech Jews also had had their *Familienlager* (Family Camp) for a long time. There, from the end of February 1943, Gypsies, the majority of whom came from Germany and Austria, had been held separate from the other prisoners in Auschwitz. A total of 22,000 Gypsies were imprisoned in the *Zigeunerlager* (Gypsy Camp) during the time of its existence. For about a year they received relatively favourable treatment.

In May 1944, however, the regime changed. After the gassing of two large groups (1,700 and over 1,000) in special actions in 1943, the Gypsies became subject to the normal rules of Auschwitz from the beginning of 1944. The strong were separated from the weak and employed in heavy *Arbeitskommandos* (work teams), sometimes transferred to other camps when needed.

By the time Theresia and Emilia Steinbach and their families arrived in Auschwitz, over a thousand prisoners had already died in the "Gypsy Camp" during the first four months of 1944, mainly from diarrhoea and typhus. By the end of July 1944, when the camp was evacuated, the Steinbachs from Holland were amongst the 6,000 or so surviving men, women and children in Lagerabschnitt B II. The liquidation of the camp took place under the pretext that typhus was rampant, and all the prisoners from Birkenau camp were at risk of infection.

The remaining Gypsies were tested for their work capacity. Boys and men strong enough to work were separated from the rest to be sent to Buchenwald; the girls and women who were fit to work went to Ravensbrück. For Toetela this meant bidding farewell to her daughters Elisabeth and Johanna Cornelia, seventeen and fourteen, and her sons Willem-Hendrik and Celestinus, nineteen and fifteen.

The two girls lost their lives in the Ravensbrück concentration camp. The exact date of their death is unknown, but the latest possible date is 24 April 1945.

Willem-Hendrik and Celestinus Steinbach, the musical brothers Elmo and Willy, went to Buchenwald concentration camp on 3rd August 1944. From Buchenwald the older brother was sent to the huge camp complex of Dora (Mittelbau) in the Harz mountains on 29 October. Willem-Hendrik Steinbach died in Block 10 of the camp in Ellrich on 28 January 1945.

His brother Celestinus was transported back to Auschwitz on 26 September with two hundred other Gypsies. Celestinus arrived in Auschwitz on 27th September and was gassed on the same day.

The two Steinbach mothers, Bütta and Toetela, and their younger children, were also murdered.

On Monday afternoon 31 July 1944, the *Zigeunerlager* was cordonned off by the SS and cleared barrack by barrack. In groups, the Gypsies were taken by freight lorries to the gas chambers of Crematorium I. The liquidation continued into the early morning of 1st August.

116

Rudolf Höss, the commandant of Auschwitz, speaks of the murder of the Gypsies in his memoirs written between his arrest and execution in 1946: "Up to the last moment they didn't know what was waiting for them. They only found out on the way to the crematorium. It was not easy to get them into the gas chamber. I did not observe it myself, but Schwarzhuber (an SS officer) told me later that not one single Jewish extermination had been as difficult as the extermination of the Gypsies. It was very hard for him because he knew them well and had a good relationship with them. Their whole manner seemed to portray a childlike trust."

The Jewish doctor Lucie Adelsberger, who worked in the children's barrack of the *Zigeunerlager*, also lived through the liquidation of the camp. She wrote later, "Slowly the freight wagons which had been going back and forth came nearer. At 22.30 they stopped in front of our barrack. Had the moment come? Our door remained closed. The lorry had not come for us but for the orphans in the barrack opposite ours. We heard the curt orders of the SS and the wails of the children. ... Half an hour later the lorries came back, to our barrack. Now it was our turn. Who would they take first, the Gypsies or the Jewish doctors? The doors were thrown open, the SS stormed in, accompanied by four prisoners. The evacuation had begun. People were pulled from their beds, picked up like bundles and carried out. We had to stand by watching helplessly. In a few minutes the barrack was empty. Each bed was ransacked again and every corner of the barrack was searched. The barrack was locked up once more and the SS went away with their victims. We remained behind unharmed. ... The following morning, 1st August, the Gypsy camp, which only the day before had held 3,500 to 4,000 people, was empty."

Of Bütta — Theresia Steinbach — it is clear that she died in one of the Auschwitz gas chambers with three of her children: the girl Walda — whose Gypsy name was Poscha —

117

and the two boys Johannes and Jean — named Sano and Tomix. The fate of her oldest son, the lame lad Karl — Tikono — is unknown.

Toetela — Emilia Steinbach — went to the gaschamber with her five youngest children, whose ages ranged from eleven to two; her sons Philibert and Willem and her daughters Anna Maria, Florentina Maria and the youngest Anna Maria.

Of all the children, the nine year old Anna Maria was to live on as a symbol and a child of the Holocaust — because as she was leaving in a goods train for Auschwitz, a German film director rested his camera on her for a moment — Settela, the girl in the door opening.

Epilogue

More than a month after my visit to the caravan park in Stein, it became clear that certain Gypsies considered that I had trodden on forbidden ground with my questions about the Steinbach family and their fate in the war.

This became evident when I phoned Toni Weiss once again, the man who on parting from me in the Rosenbergs' caravan, had willingly given me his telephone number in case I wanted to know anything else. I wanted to ask Toni Weiss if I could visit him in Stein to talk to him again. I also wanted to tell him that Cherry Duyns, a documentary film maker for the national television station VPRO, would like to film the story of my quest for Settela, and wanted to talk to Weiss, the fount of so much knowledge.

But the Toni Weiss who now answered the telephone was a completely different man from the self-assured, eloquent and expansive narrator I had met on that cold February day, sprinkling his plentiful chronicles of Gypsy life with colourful anecdotes. I now heard the voice of a timid, awkward man on the line, curtly trying to tell me that he didn't want to converse with me any more.

I was startled by this. Toni Weiss heard or felt this and was then nice enough to explain this sudden embargo. He said: "You were really very lucky, the day you were with us!"

Then he told me that less than quarter of an hour after I had left the Veestraat, a man from the Steinbach family had visited the Rosenbergs. News spreads so quickly in the Gypsy community that he had got wind of the fact that a gentleman from The Hague was enquiring about members of his family.

When he found out that his family had been the sole topic of conversation in the Rosenbergs' caravan for almost three hours, and that to make matters worse, Kercheman had come round with a few family photos, this

119

man — Veigli he was called, one of Moeselman's nephews — had flown into a great rage and cursed everyone and everything in the camp on the Veestraat.

A Gypsy does not act like that, he reproached them violently; you never speak to outsiders about members of someone else's family. And especially not when those Gypsies are dead and — as is the case of Moeselman and his wife and children — have been murdered or have died of grief!

"You will never hear from us again," said Toni Weiss, "and you must never approach the Steinbachs. You would be kicked out of the camp!"

I never endured such an experience because I simply never again came close to visiting the Steinbachs in their caravan parks in Stein, Valkenburg, Gulpen, Maasbracht or anywhere else. Weiss's bleak prophecy was true: a high wall of secrecy had been erected round the Gypsy community of Zuid Limburg.

When I phoned any Steinbachs whose phone numbers I had found, the receiver was slammed down immediately I gave my name. And when I approached members of other Gypsy families, they were friendly, but stubbornly refused to arrange a conversation with the Steinbachs on my behalf.

One of them was forthcoming enough to explain the almost Old Testament ban that existed amongst the Gypsies about looking back and speaking of the dead. "You surely know about Lot — in spite of being forbidden to do so, his wife looked back and was turned into a pillar of salt."

Any further search for Settela — for her roots, how she had lived her short life, and what had happened to her after the wagon doors of the train had been shut in Westerbork — I would now have to pursue from the periphery of the Gypsy community.

Over the next few months I contacted — either making personal visits or by telephone — town and regional archivists, priests, nuns from a Belgian Gypsy pastorate,

120

teachers and civil servants of the villages and towns of South Limburg.

I went on a study pilgrimage to the chapel outside the Limburg city of Roermond, where the wooden statue of Onze Lieve Vrouwe in 't Zand (Our Holy Lady in the Sand) is to be found and where for centuries, Gypsies have come to offer prayers and honour Maria. I visited the Overmaas cemetery on the borders of Maastricht, where in section 053, behind a conifer hedge, Moeselman's grave lies, and looked at the high white marble headstone with its golden image of the Virgin Mary beneath a black painting of two violins with bows. Two white marble doves sit on the edge of the grave.

"Here lies Heinrich Steinbach 11 November 1902 — 9th June 1946."

During this period, I retrieved from the basements of town halls and village municipalities, the birth certificates of all the young members of the twenty-six Steinbachs who had died in the war. In this way I figured out the composition of the family of Moeselman and Toetela or, as they were entered in the public registry, Heinrich Steinbach and Emilia Steinbach-Steinbach.

They had ten children. The oldest was Magadelena Gertruda, born in Brunssum in 1922. The youngest child, a second Anna Maria, was born in Linne in 1942. The middle children were Willem-Hendrik, 1925, Brunssum; Elisabeth, 1926, Meerssen; Celestinus, 1929, Heerlen; Johanna Cornelia, 1930, Maastricht; Philibert, 1932, Geleen; Anna Maria, 1934, Born; Florentina Maria, 1937, Sittard; Willem, 1939, Sittard.

The day arrived when I was finally convinced that Anna Maria Steinbach, born in Buchten in the department of Born on 23rd December 1934, was the girl who the Gypsies called Settela.

A lot of reflection and deliberation preceded my conclusion. All the same I could not find any hard evidence. But

121

I did keep gathering more and more clues which strengthened my conviction that Settela, the girl in the door opening of the train wagon, was born Anna Maria Steinbach and was inscribed with that name in the *Remembrance Book* of the War Graves' Foundation.

She was the only one of Emilia Steinbach's daughters who could have been called Settela. After all, Crasa Wagner had made it clear that Settela had remained in Auschwitz with her mother on the day that the older Gypsy women, like Crasa herself and Magdalena Berger, were deemed suitable for what Crasa called the *Arbeitseinsatz*; transportation to the concentration camp of Ravensbrück in Mecklenburg, North Germany.

I already knew that two of Toetela's daughters, Elizabeth (1926) and Johanna Cornelia (1930), were also amongst the group of older Gypsy girls sent from Auschwitz to Ravensbrück.

In addition, I knew that Toetela's oldest child, Magdalena Gertruda (1922), was no longer living with her family in 1944, nor was she amongst the Gypsies who left Westerbork by train on May 19 1944.

Of Toetela's three other daughters, Florentina Maria, who was seven when she left Westerbork, and Anna Maria, who was two, did not fall into the age range in which Crasa Wagner had put Settela. "About eleven years old," the woman in Spijkenisse had told me.

There was still another girl from the families of Theresia and Emilia Steinbach who was in the correct age group, and who had also died in Auschwitz; Walda (1930). But Walda's Gypsy name, so I learnt, was Poscha.

Anna Maria, born in 1934, was the only possible candidate; she must have been the girl who heard her mother yell at her that she should be careful as she stood at the closing doors of the wagon; "Settela, get away from that door, otherwise your head will get stuck!"

The most moving document I found regarding Moeselman and Toetela Steinbach and their children, was in the

122

Information Office of the Dutch Red Cross in The Hague. From the archives a pile of files appeared in light brown wrapping paper; dossiers dating from 1945 and 1946. The thickest file was that of Emilia Steinbach, Gypsy name Toetela, and the other dossiers were about the children, one little folder for each of the ten.

My guide in the archives, familiar with the average bulk of the more than one hundred thousand "search dossiers" which have been kept by the Red Cross since 1945, mumbled in admiration, "The father, Heinrich Steinbach, did quite a bit of work; he turned to nearly every institution that existed, those first months after the liberation."

Heinrich Steinbach, Moeselman, had been illiterate. And the person who helped him search in 1945 and 1946 by filling in forms for him, was barely literate. He wrote Heinrich's forename in faltering letters as "Henderik," stated his religion as "Catholic" and his profession as "musician", mispelling the Dutch words as *Katelik* and *muziekant*, instead of *Katholiek* and *muzicant*. It is evident from his tracing application that Moeselman suspected his wife and children had been sent to a *"konterasiekamp"* (*concentratiecamp*), apparently in *"Ausswits in Poollen's"* instead of *"Auschwitz in Polen"*.

When his wife and children were taken from the collection camp in Eindhoven on 16 May 1944, Heinrich Steinbach himself had already been imprisoned for a week. He had been picked up with his two brothers Wilhelmus — Koleman — and Hendrik — Rico — and another four adult Gypsies, and dispatched to the concentration camp of Amersfoort.

On 25 May a large transport travelled out of the Amersfoort camp; 1,648 Dutch men were sent to work camps in Düsseldorf and Wuppertal. Heinrich Steinbach, however, did not go with them. He was transferred to Camp Westerbork with the other Gypsies a few days later. There Moeselman and Koleman heard that their wives

123

and children had been transported by train to Auschwitz in Poland on 19 May.

A short time later, Moeselman and the other Gypsies were sent back from Westerbork to Eindhoven, where they were set to work at the Philips' factories. Following 17th September 1944, when the Allies liberated Eindhoven, Heinrich Steinbach chose to make his home in the caravan park of the Zwaaikampstraat. The first time Moeselman made an enquiry about his family from that address was on 9th March 1945, even before the whole of Holland had been liberated. His request was directed to the Dutch mission in Paris.

My guide and I opened the files and scattered the cards and drafts, the forms and the letters, some handwritten, some typed, onto the table. In a cloud of dust lay the material evidence that half a century ago, the girl Florentina Maria Steinbach, nickname Sonja, had existed; she had been seven years old and categorised as "a Gypsy/ political prisoner" when she died in Auschwitz. Next to her records I saw those of Willem Steinbach, called Messelo, not quite five years old when, on arrival in Auschwitz on May 22nd 1944, the *Häftlingnummer* Z10017 had been tattoed on his arm. The youngest child, Anna Maria, nickname Doosje, was two years old when she too, was killed as a "Gypsy/political prisoner."

I browsed through the file of Elisabeth Steinbach, born 14 November 1926, who had arrived in Auschwitz on 22 May 1944. Written on one of the cards was the note, "In connection with work capacity possible 1-8-1944 to Ravensbrück". I found the same words in the dossier of Johanna Cornelia Steinbach, born 18 March 1930. On her card was scribbled in small letters: "Latest possible date of death 24-4-1945." On or around that day in April 1945, Russian soldiers reached Ravensbrück and found the concentration camp largely evacuated.

In the files of Willem-Hendrik and Celestinus Steinbach, Emilia and Heinrich's two eldest sons, there were scaled-down photocopies of their identity cards from Buchenwald concentration camp, where the brothers arrived on 3rd August 1944, after having been separated from their mother and siblings in Auschwitz.

I read on Willem-Hendrik's card, (tattoo left arm Z10016), that he was 1.63 meters tall and of *schwächlich* (puny) build. His face was angular, his nose *etwa gebogen* (somewhat curved) and he had brown eyes and black hair. His brother Celestinus (Z10019), four years younger, was much smaller, 1.50 metres. According to the card from Buchenwald, he had an oval face, slightly protruding ears, his own set of teeth, black hair and brown eyes. Both the Steinbach brothers had *Musiker* (musician) as profession on their cards, and furthermore the note that they were *Arbeitsscheu* (Workshy).

It took me the afternoon and part of the evening to leaf through and read the search dossiers, which had got thicker and thicker in the years following Heinrich Steinbach's search in 1945 and 1946. The final request for information dates from 1976 and was directed to the *Internationale Suchdienst* (International Search Service) in the German town of Arolsen.

We sometimes came across facts in the files — names and dates — that did not agree with each other. For example, Elisabeth, instead of having her birth date noted as 14 November 1926, was given the birth date 28 August 1939, which belonged to her brother Willem. On one occasion, Willem-Hendrik was omitted from a list of the missing children. The compiler of two other lists — written in English for the benefit of international search agencies — showed that Heinrich Steinbach had given the names and birthdates of nine out of ten of his missing children, omitting the name of Anna Maria, born 23 December 1934.

She — the girl I have designated as Settela — was inscribed in the documents as: "and a child whose name he cannot remember." But ten months after the war the name of that child did come back to him, after all. On 14th

March 1946, Heinrich added the forgotten child to the list of his beloved missing relations; she was called Anna Maria and according to Heinrich's statement, had been born on 23 December 1934 in the village of Buchten. As for her "nickname/Gypsy name" Heinrich suddenly remembered the name "Blieta."

Blieta?

Not Settela?

On 22 May 1946, with the help of the Maastricht Advice Bureau of the Communist Party and its daily paper, *De Waarheid* (The Truth), Heinrich Steinbach once more made enquiries about those members of his family who had been transported from Westerbork. In his letter he mentions the names and birth dates of his wife Emilia, his six daughters and four sons. He could only remember the Gypsy names of his oldest daughter and his four youngest children; "Mokkela" for Magdalena Gertruda (1922), "Doosje" for Anna Maria (1942), "Messelo" for Willem (1939), "Sonja" for Florentina Maria (1937) and "Blieta" for Anna Maria (1934).

The Gypsy name "Settela" does not appear in the letter. Nor does the name "Elmo" — as the left handed musical crown prince, Moeselman's oldest son Willem-Hendrik was known. The name "Willy", by which his younger brother Celestinus is still remembered, is also absent.

The tracing request of 22 May 1946 was Heinrich Steinbach's last attempt to get his wife and children back. Two and a half weeks later, on 9 June 1946, he died, aged forty-four, in a caravan in the little camp at the Gerardusweg in Maastricht. According to those who knew him in his last few months, Moeselman was very confused and sometimes mad with grief. Did Settela's name elude him in that state of mind?

As I left the Red Cross building on the evening of 14 July 1994, I felt that my search had come to an end. I had not been able to get any closer to the identity of the girl in the

126

Auschwitz train. The brown folder belonging to Anna Maria, born 23 December 1934 in Buchten, was one of the slenderest in the heap of Red Cross files relating to the murdered Gypsy family from Limburg. Initially given the number 42496, the dossier was later altered to 144903. The most recent addition is a pencil scribble saying that the name of Anna Maria Steinbach was "removed from the Central Register of Population" on 14 May 1947.

Afterword

Romanies in the Netherlands during the Holocaust
Ian Hancock

Romanies[1], commonly but inaccurately called *Gypsies*, were the only other population besides the Jews who were targeted for extermination on racial grounds in the Final Solution. They arrived in Europe about the year 1300 from India, which they had left nearly three centuries before as a military population of mixed ethnic origin assembled to fight the invading Muslims, or else themselves serving as contingents of the Muslim armies (Hancock, 2004, Marsh, 2005). Their entry into Europe, via the Byzantine Empire, was also the direct result of Islamic expansion.

---

[1]Settela was a Sinti Romani. Accounts of the Holocaust often refer to its Romani victims as "Sinti and Roma", which has caused journalists and others considerable confusion. Although *Roma* is being increasingly used as the correct ethnic label for the Romani people, not all — the Sinti — call themselves that. All groups, however, are comfortable with the adjective *Romani* to describe themselves, so while Sinti will protest at being called Roma, they will nevertheless call themselves Romani people. *Romani*, plural *Romanies*, is used here to refer to all people of Romani descent. All Romani populations regard death and the souls of the deceased with great reverence. It is widely felt that dwelling on the Holocaust is a bad thing, because the *mulé*—the spirits of those murdered—should be left in peace. In Sinti homes in particular, speaking the names of deceased family members is avoided, and their pictures may be turned to the wall or draped with a cloth. For this reason, Romanies have generally been less strident in demanding full recognition of their fate in the Holocaust, and survivors have been reluctant to share their experiences with modern-day chroniclers. Some families have refused even to accept small sums offered as war crimes reparation, because of its association with the "devouring of life" (the *Porrajmos*) as the Holocaust is called in Vlax Romani.

As a non-Christian, non-white, Asian people possessing no territory in Europe, Romanies were outsiders in everybody's country. Their culture also ensured — as it still does — that a social distance be kept between Romanies and *gadjé* (non-Romanies), and thus their separateness was further reinforced.

Romani people in the northern countries of Europe call themselves Sinti, while *Zigeuner* is the equivalent of "Gypsy" in both Dutch and German, and is no longer a politically correct term. When the Nazis came to power in 1933, German laws against Romanies had already been in effect for hundreds of years. The persecution of the Romani people began almost as soon as they first arrived in German-speaking lands because as outsiders, they were breaking many of the Hanseatic laws which made it a punishable offence not to have a permanent home or job, and not to be on the taxpayer's register. They were also accused of being spies for the Muslims, whom few northern Europeans had ever met but about whom they had heard many frightening stories. The dark complexions and non-Christian behaviour and appearance of the Romanies simply added to the prejudice that was steadily growing. In 1721 Emperor Karl VI ordered the extermination of all Romanies everywhere; it was not illegal to murder them, and during that period the Dutch government periodically ordered "Gypsy hunts", in which the police were empowered to round up and drive Romanies out of the country, mostly into Germany. Forests were even set on fire to force out any Romanies who might have been hiding there. By the 19th Century, scholars in Germany and elsewhere in Europe were writing about Romanies as being inferior beings, and "the excrement of humanity." This crystallised into specifically racist attitudes in the writing of Knox, Tetzner, Gobineau and others. By the 1880s, Chancellor von Bismarck reinforced some of the discriminatory laws, stating that Romanies were to be dealt with "especially severely" if apprehended. In or around 1890, a conference on "The Gypsy Scum" was held in Swabia, at which the military was empowered to keep Romanies on the move. In 1899 Houston Chamberlaine's work *The Foundations of the 19th Century* was published, which argued for the building of a "newly shaped ... and ... especially deserving Aryan race." It was used to justify the promotion of ideas about German racial superiority, and for any oppressive action taken against members of "inferior" populations. In that same year, the "Gypsy Information Agency" was set up in Munich under the direction of Alfred Dillmann, which began cataloguing information on all Romanies throughout the German lands. The results of this were published in 1905 in Dillmann's *Zigeuner-Buch*, which laid the foundations for what was to befall Romanies in the Holocaust 35 years later.

The *Zigeuner-Buch*, nearly 350 pages long, consisted of three parts: first, an introduction stating that Romanies were a "plague" and a "menace" which the German population had to defend itself against using "ruthless punishments", and which warned of the dangers of mixing the Romani and German gene pools. The second part was a register of known Romanies, giving genealogical details and criminal record if any, and the third part was a collection of photographs of those same people. Dillmann's "race mixing" later became a central part of the Nuremberg Law in Nazi Germany.

In 1920, Karl Binding and Alfred Hoche published their book *The Eradication of Lives Undeserving of Life*, using a phrase first coined by Richard Liebich with specific reference to Romanies nearly sixty years earlier. Among the groups they considered "unworthy of life" were the "incurably mentally ill", and it was to this group that Romanies were considered to belong. Perceived Romani "criminality" was seen as a transmitted genetic disease, though no account was taken of the centuries of exclusion of the Romanies from German society, which made subsistence theft a necessity for survival. A law incorporating the same phrase was put into effect just four months after Hitler became Chancellor of the Third Reich.

During the 1920s the legal oppression of Romanies in Germany intensified considerably, despite the egalitarian statutes of the Weimar Republic. In 1920 they were forbidden to enter parks and public baths; in 1925 a conference on "The Gypsy Question" was held which resulted in laws requiring unemployed Romanies to be sent to work camps "for reasons of public security", and for all Romanies to be registered with the police. After 1927, all Romanies, even children, had to carry identification cards, bearing fingerprints and photographs. In 1929, The Central Office for the Fight Against the Gypsies in Germany was established in Munich, and in 1933, just ten days before the Nazis came to power, government officials in Burgenland called for the withdrawal of all civil rights from the Romani people.

In September 1935 Romanies became subject to the restrictions of the Nuremberg Law for the Protection of German Blood and Honor, which forbade intermarriage between Germans and "non-Aryans," specifically Romanies, Jews and people of African descent. In 1937, the National Citizenship Law relegated Romanies and Jews to the status of second-class citizens, depriving them of their civil rights. Also in 1937, Heinrich Himmler issued a decree entitled "The Struggle Against the Gypsy Plague", which reiterated that Romanies of mixed blood were the most likely to engage in criminal activity, and which required that all information on Romanies be sent from the regional police departments to the Reich Central Office.

The first document referring to "the introduction of the total solution to the Gypsy problem on either a national or an international level" was issued under the direction of State Secretary Hans Pfundtner of the Reichs Ministry of the Interior in March, 1936, while the wording *endgültige Lösung der Zigeunerfrage*, i.e. the "final (or 'conclusive') solution of the Gypsy question", appeared in print in a directive signed by Himmler in May, 1938. Between June 12th and June 18th that same year, *Gypsy Clean-Up Week* took place throughout Germany which, like Kristallnacht for the Jewish people in November that year, marked the beginning of the end.

In January, 1940, the. first mass genocidal action of the Holocaust took place when 250 Romani children were murdered in Buchenwald, where they were used as guinea-pigs to test the efficacy of the Zyklon-B crystals, later used in the gas chambers. In June the same year, Hitler ordered the liquidation of "all Jews, Gypsies and communist political functionaries in the entire Soviet Union."

On July, 31st 1941, Heydrich, chief architect of the details of the Final Solution, issued his directive to the *Einsatzkommandos* to "kill all Jews, Gypsies and mental patients." A few days later Himmler issued his criteria for biological and racial evaluation, which determined that each Rom's family background was to be investigated going back three generations. On December 16th that same year, Himmler issued the order to have all Romanies remaining in Europe deported to Auschwitz-Birkenau for extermination. On December 24th, Lohse gave the additional order that "The Gypsies should be given the same treatment as the Jews." At a party meeting on September 14th, 1942, Justice Minister Otto Thierack announced that "Jews and Gypsies must be unconditionally exterminated." On August 1st, 1944, four thousand Romanies were gassed and cremated in a single action at Auschwitz-Birkenau, in what is remembered as *Zigeunernacht*.

By 1942 the Dutch press had begun to intensify its anti-Romani propaganda; in June the *Nord-Brabantsche Courant* wrote of a "plague" of Gypsies descending upon the provinces of Limburg and Brabant and causing great public nuisance, and called for a central, police-run site to contain all Romanies throughout the country. This was established at Westerbork under the command of SS-Obersturmführer Albert Konrad Gemmeker , and following a special police action Romanies living in the Netherlands were incarcerated there. On March 29th the following year, Himmler ordered their deportation to Auschwitz where 245 souls — including Anna Maria Steinbach — *Settela* — arrived on May 21st. There were about 300 Dutch Romanies in Auschwitz altogether. Practically all of the Romani population in the Netherlands had been removed; some individuals may have been taken in and hidden by the *Woonwagenbewooners*, the non-Romani Travellers in the Netherlands, others may have ended up in work camps, and one group managed to escape to Guatemala. But out of a 1939 national population of five hundred practically all had perished by 1945.

The Netherlands' treatment of Romanies since that time has been recognized as among the more progressive in post-war Europe (Kenrick & Puxon, 1972:199). As early as 1948 a government proposal recommended the creation of a network of sites for Romanies and *Woonwagenbewooners* throughout the country, although it was another decade before they began to build, in cooperation with local authorities, the first of eight camps (at Hertogenbosch). Since then more have been provided, some of which have nursery Montessori schools attached. At last report, fewer than half of the Romani and Traveller families in the Netherlands are established in such premises. As elsewhere, antigypsyism remains a reality, thus in the mid 1990s an empty house in Utrecht which was being remodelled for a Romani family with two children was trashed by vandals, who were never caught, while at the same time individuals from the same neighborhood interviewed by the press claimed that Romanies "disturb the peace." With the fall of communism in 1989 and new central and eastern European countries joining the European Union, the anticipated movement West of increasing numbers of Romanies will surely keep alive issues of integration to the Netherlands' multi-ethnic society.

Further reading

1. Hancock, Ian, 1989. "Gypsy history in Germany and neighboring lands: a chronology leading to the Holocaust and beyond," in David Crowe and John Kolsti (eds.), *The Gypsies of Eastern Europe*, Armonk: E.C. Sharpe, pp. 11-30.
2. Hancock, Ian, 2004. "Romanies and the Holocaust: a re-evaluation and an overview," in Dan Stone (ed.) *The Historiography of the Holocaust*, New York: Palgrave-Macmillan, pp. 383-396.
3. Hancock, Ian, 2004. "On Romani origins and identity," in Adrian Marsh & Elin Strand (eds.), *Contextual, Constructed and Contested: Gypsies and the Problem of Identities*. Transactions of the Swedish Research Institute in Istanbul No. 13. Malmö and Istanbul, pp. 5-23.
4. Kenrick, Donald, and Puxon, Grattan, 1972. *The Destiny of Europe's Gypsies,* London: Sussex University Press.
5. Marsh, Adrian, 2005. *History, Historiography and Identity; Gypsies in the Late Ottoman Empire.* Unpublished doctoral dissertation, London: Greenwich University.

Reviews of Dutch Edition of Settela

If the name of Anne Frank is the most famous of the Shoah, then Settela — the girl between the doors of a cattle wagon departing from Westerbork to Auschwitz — is the most well-known face. The head scarf, her half open mouth, her lonely scared eyes. Those seven seconds that have been seen so often, but which never fail to disturb. Wagenaar started to look for the identity of this girl who symbolises the murder of six million Jews, but who turned out to be a Gypsy. His dogged search, exemplifying superior journalism, is the shocking story of that section of the population who suffered their heavy losses in silence and who, in silence, carry their burden with them.
Rob Hartmans in *Hervormd Nederland*

...Wagenaar shows himself to be a dogged investigator and an excellent reporter. He reveals how much effort his research cost him, he relates his conversations with camp victims and historians, and details his studies of all the documents available. (...) It appears that Wagenaar, possessed by feelings of horror and pity, used all his ingenuity to pursue his search. He wanted to give the girl back her name. And though this serves nobody, it is as if justice has been done. A very moving book...
Alfred Kossman in *Arnhemsche Courant*

One of the most remarkable books of late is *Settela*. In it, journalist Aad Wagenaar compellingly reports his search for the identity of the girl in the world-famous film excerpt: a girl with a head scarf who looks from between the doors of a train wagon, just before the train sets off to the extermination camps...
Han van Gessel in *De Volkskrant*

Wagenaar's book is not only the story of a fascination, but a bitter reminder of another file (dossier) of Nazi genocide.

This one is less known and has thus been underestimated. The Gypsies have been marginalized, stigmatised, exploited and persecuted throughout the ages. They are prevented by their culture from asking for recognition and compensation for their wartime misery from those by whom they are marginalised and seen as scapegoats. And then there is the fact that they want to cope with their wartime family experiences and their lost ones within an intimate circle. Outsiders are not welcome. Aad Wagenaar has experienced this too...
Johan de Roey in *De Hoogste Tijd*

Wagenaar's book *Settela* is a mixture of the horror endured by Jews and Gypsies during the war, and the fanatical search of a journalist seeking the identity of the girl. The story is impressive and stirring, and grips the reader to the last page...
Menno Schenken in *Algemeen Dagblad*

Wagenaar has succeeded in correcting one of the many major and minor misunderstandings that sneak into the valid picture of the Holocaust. His book is not only meant as a historical correction, but is also an attempt to draw attention to a lesser known group of victims...
Georgi Verbeeck in *De Standaard*, Brussels

Wagenaar's long and tenacious research demanded from him an intimate knowledge of men, the patience of a monk, and impressive professional zeal. He has put the spotlight on another aspect of the *Endlösung*, the mass murder of the Gypsies which remained virtually unpublicised for many years after the war. The historical facts, as well as the sensitive way that Wagenaar describes his search, make this book a moving read...
Jos van Damme in *Leesidee*